Today and Tomorrow

Today and Tomorrow

By
Edgar A. Guest

The Reilly & Lee Co.
Chicago

*Dedicated to America
and to All Americans*

—EDGAR A. GUEST

INDEX

Index

Index

Index

Index

Index

TOMORROW

Always and ever tomorrow,
  The day of our hopes and our dreams;
The end of all failure and sorrow
  How close and how far off it seems!
Tomorrow—the goal a day nearer!
  Tomorrow—one day farther on
The way just a little bit clearer
  And some old discouragement gone!

Always and ever before us
  Tomorrow holds promises fair,
Life just a bit easier for us
  And lighter its burdens to bear.
Tomorrow—then loosened some fetter,
  Some evil of old set aright
Life richer and gayer and better.
  Tomorrow—just after tonight.

Tomorrow with beauty of morning
  And evening and nighttime and noon.
Tomorrow—the better day dawning
  For all of us, later or soon.
Long yesterdays over and ended
  Lie down with the past in the grave
But forever to victories splendid
  Tomorrow will welcome the brave.

MANHOOD

Whatever change the future brings,
　　Honor and pluck will be required.
These to the end of earthly things
　　Will be respected and desired.

Let isms flourish as they may,
　　He will be numbered with the few
Who shows a willingness to stay,
　　And fight his difficulties through.

There will be need and praise for skill
　　And skill by patience comes alone!
By all we judge as good and ill
　　Will man's accomplishments be known.

No law can lessen wisdom's price,
　　Or easier make the heights to climb,
Success will call for sacrifice
　　In toil and study, faith and time.

Oh, eager youth be not misled!
　　Long is the road to decent fame.
Whatever changes lie ahead
　　The cost of manhood stays the same.

ONE FOR ALL

What if we differed yesterday, with danger at the
    door,
We're one and all for one and all, the family whole
    once more;
We like to argue this and that and question pro and
    con,
But trouble finds us one for all and all of us for one.

We'll quarrel some in days of peace, but don't be
    fooled by that,
Don't think the family's broken when we knock each
    other flat;
For should some bully come along and strike our
    youngster small,
Before he'd launch a second blow he'd have to fight
    us all.

We're full of sects and creeds and groups, with no-
    tions old and new,
And some like this and some like that and part, as
    families do;
But though we differ 'mong ourselves, when backed
    against the wall,
You'll always find us all for one and every one for all.

JEALOUS

In the happy days gone by
Never jealous—much—was I.
Bolder men, and handsomer, too,
Came at times and tried to woo,
But her heart to me was true
And she laughed away the lot.
So back then I worried not.

Then I thought—but I was wrong—
There will never come along
Rival, blue of eye and fair,
Plump of cheek and brown of hair,
Love all mine to steal or share;
One with whom by night or day
She will think to run away.

But he's here and off she goes,
Leaving me to sit and doze.
Off she flies and answers: "Nay!"
When I beg of her to stay.
"Love is luring me away!
Love has captivated me!
'Tis with him I long to be."

So I stay at home and doze!
'Tis what happens, I suppose,
Unto all men, weather-worn

Like old volumes, soiled and torn,
On the day a grandson's born!
Every grandpa must retreat
From a rival he can't beat.

❧   ❧   ❧

"FLAG OF THE GREAT IDEA"

"Flag of the Great Idea!" Whitman penned.
Flag of the mother, father, brother, friend!
Flag of the dream of everlasting good,
Banner of right and peace and brotherhood.

Brave flag, of the remaining very few
To liberty and all its teaching true!
Bright flag of hope for all the world's distressed,
Riding the breeze for everything that's best.

Flag of the Great Idea 'gainst the sky,
Symbol of hope for every passerby.
Born of a dream and to the dream still true,
Banner of freedom! red and white and blue.

TWILIGHT

Closed office and shop,
  Shut foundry and mill;
Trade's bickerings stop
  And the city turns still.
For tired eyes like mine
  At the edge of the town,
There is drama divine
  As the sun's going down.

The smoke of the day,
  The grinding of gears,
The laughter of play
  And the little folks' tears
Have all ceased as the night
  Sings: "Enough! Come to rest."
And the sun slips from sight,
  Molten gold in the west.

And I think as I stand
  For a moment in awe
Of the work of God's hand
  Which Adam first saw,
And the last will behold
  At the long day's decline.
For all eyes, young or old,
  Here is drama divine!

IN PERPETUITY

Continuous and perpetual stay
The red geraniums, come what may
Not all man's hate nor all his greed
Can kill the life in poppy seed,
Or check the blossoms as they come
To peony and delphinium.

Man's finest structures through the night
Fall prey to warfare's dynamite,
And any skillful enemy
Can sink his stoutest ships at sea.
War leaves in rubble desolate
All that his genius can create.

But all unguarded in the sun
On walls and trellis ivies run.
In dread of neither gas nor shell
Blossoms the Canterbury bell;
And never any rosebush grows
In terror of another rose.

The things the hand of man creates
Are subject always to his hates
And from the earth may disappear,
But still, forever, year by year,
Will be repeated as of old
The bloom of phlox and marigold.

MOTHER COURAGE

And still she smiles with us today
  And bravely does her share,
Although her boy has gone away
  And may not tell her where.
And still she hums a cheerful song
  And shows no sign of dread,
But marches, just as he, along
  The path that all must tread.

Day after day she carries fear
  Deep hidden in her heart;
And with unbounded courage here
  Contrives to do her part.
She reads his penciled *"All is well,"*
  News censors grave prefer,
And writes at once to him to tell,
  That all is well with her.

These days are hard for mothers all,
  Whose boys have marched away.
They never hear the bugle call,
  On guard at home are they.
And oh, how brave and fine they are,
  The long suspense to bear,
Whose boys are absent and afar
  And may not tell them where!

FISHING THOUGHT

Wish I were the president, twice a year or so
Out upon a battleship fishing I would go.
"Call me up a cruiser," now and then I'd say.
"From these office seekers I must get away."

Wish I were the president! miles and miles at sea,
Where there are no telephones, fishing I would be.
Right this very moment I would whisper low:
"Ring me up a battleship; fishing I would go."

Wish I were the president! Wouldn't it be great?
Sailors hoisting anchor; sailors passing bait!
If the boat be leaky, sailorboys to bail,
And, what's even better, cooks to clean and scale.

Wish I were the president! No, I take it back!
Far too many burdens fill his daily pack.
Even when he's fishing, problems fret his mind.
Rather be the fellow who must stay behind.

TOLERATION

If life were as simple as a, b, c,
As easy to see through as 1, 2, 3;
If good and bad were as clear as day,
And foolish and wise the selfsame way,
Then truly I'd cherish the good and wise
And all that is foolish and bad despise.

If I could be certain that all is truth
That was taught to me in my early youth;
If right and wrong were as day and night,
As clear to the eye as black and white,
I'd stone whatever of wrong I found
And build my dwelling on holy ground.

If I could be certain my chosen creed
Is the only one that all mortals need,
I'd frown on others. But who can say
That his to Heaven is the only way?
So I try to live with an open mind
And look for the best in whatever I find.

LINCOLN'S BIRTHDAY

We stand at Gettysburg today
  As Lincoln stood of old,
And need a Lincoln now to say
  The truths men should be told,
Lest unreminded we may stray
  From faiths that all should hold.

Would he were here once more to pen
  In simple phrase and pure
A thought to rally faltering men
  To truths which should endure;
Reconsecrating us again
  Till freedom's cause is sure.

We are the living, as he said,
  Now say it once again!
Ours are the great tasks just ahead.
  Steadfast must we remain
To freedom's purpose, that our dead
  Shall not have died in vain.

WHAT KIND OF PEOPLE

They have thought us easy-going. We've been that
    beyond a doubt.
Now they'll learn, since they've attacked us, thick or
    thin, we stick it out.
They have thought us money-grubbers and have
    sneered at us for that,
But they'll change their minds about us when it comes
    our turn to bat.

They have said we loved our comforts far too much
    to want to fight;
That we planned for peace and friendship, and in
    saying that were right,
For until that fatal morning, when behind our backs
    they struck,
We had wanted no occasion to display our brand of
    pluck.

What kind of people are we? Let us answer one and
    all;
The kind of people willing to respond to duty's call,
The kind that hates injustice and will battle hard and
    long
To smash all evil forces and make right what's plainly
    wrong.

They have sneered at us for sleeping when we should
    have been awake.

They have jeered at us for keeping all the promises
we make.
Well, we've promised all deliverance from the vicious
tyrant hordes,
And until we've kept that promise we shall never
sheathe our swords.

Let us shout it to their faces, they shall sneer at us
no more.
We shall track them down the oceans and shall dog
them on the shore,
Wheresoe'er they slink for safety, we shall follow day
and night
Until men are freed forever from the tyranny of
might.

ADORED FAMILIARITY

The days are growing longer now,
  The frozen earth is out of bond,
And yields unto the turning plow.
  The warm breeze ripples pool and pond
And yesterday the mothering earth
The first new snowdrop brought to birth.

How old this repetition seems!
  Ever and ever bud and leaf
And bird-call by the silver streams,
  How old and beautiful and brief!
And still how new seems everything
Which makes the splendor of the spring.

'Twas so a thousand years ago
  And will be so with each return.
Another thousand years will know
  Tulip and daffodil and fern.
The sweet arbutus, commonplace,
The breast of mother earth will grace.

And should there be a million springs,
  The last of them will still repeat
The glory of familiar things
  As these which make our season sweet:
Warm earth, green leaves and petals bright,
Trees filled with song and birds in flight.

SUM OF THE YEARS

What more has life to offer when you count its
    splendors o'er,
Than a loved one's kiss of welcome as you step inside
    your door?
Do you know a richer treasure, as you run earth's
    treasures through,
Than the laughter of your children and their pride
    in all you do?

Though the dictionary fortune is of lands and stocks
    and gold,
There's a deeper vein of riches, cherished highly
    though untold;
And a neighbor's good opinion and a friend's devo-
    tion true
Must be counted in the record of the things you gain
    or do.

There's the help you've been to others and the gifts
    of time and strength,
And the service to your country, through a lifetime's
    breadth and length.
There's the home! From needless heartache did you
    spare it best you could?
Well, that's all life has to offer—that's success and
    fortune good.

"WE INTERRUPT!"

"We interrupt the program!" all day long we
    heard the cry,
"To announce that England's bravest have been
    ordered out to die!
"We interrupt the program!" and the merry music
    stopped,
"To announce on frightened people bombs of death
    are being dropped."

In our happy, peaceful country this we heard the
    whole day long,
Stopping morning prayer and sermon, noon-day
    talk and evening song,
"We interrupt the program!" so that all the world
    may hear
"The sirens telling London German planes are
    drawing near."

"We interrupt the program!" and I thought how
    wise the phrase!
That's what war has done for ages in a thousand
    dreadful ways.
Art and faith and skill and science all have had
    their dreams delayed
And their programs interrupted while a war was
    being made.

Song has ceased and mirth has ended, from the
    useful forge and loom

Men are called to fill the trenches in the senseless
   fields of doom.
Now this hateful interruption falls upon the world
   again,
Destroying and delaying all the nobler aims of men.

❧ ❧ ❧

SOUL THINGS

All these are evidence of things divine:
The tulip bed; the ampelopsis vine;
The marigold of summer, and the grass
Kept green to glad the eyes of all who pass.

The white, trim curtains at the window pane
Tell something more than speech can quite explain.
The clean-swept walk; the painted boards anew—
Tasks which the flesh is not required to do.

No law demands; no force there is compels
Adornment of the spot where mortal dwells;
Brutes are content where plenty is to feed,
The love of beauty is a higher need.

We prove our souls by little things like these:
Beds of blue larkspur, phlox, anemones;
Curtains of lace; arm chairs at blazing fires
And bits of beauty more than flesh requires.

SIGNS

When they start in being good,
Doing everything they should;
When their "yes sirs" and their "pleases"
Are remembered night and day;
When with nothing further said
They go willingly to bed,
They've discovered Christmas morning
Isn't very far away.

When, should "no" be your reply
They no longer question "why?"
When they keep their noses "tidy,"
As my mother used to say;
When attempts to comb their hair
Uncomplainingly they bear;
Those are signs that Christmas morning
Isn't very far away.

When the little girls and boys
Nightly put away their toys
And they come without rebelling
When you call them in from play;
When at table it is seen
They have washed until they're clean!
They've discovered Christmas morning
Isn't very far away.

HOME

"This is where we live," said she,
  "Where we live and where we die;
This is where at rest are we
  While the world goes rushing by;
This is where, in idle hours,
We meet birds and bees and flowers.

"Here we put the shams aside;
  Here the day begins and ends;
Here our gifts are all untied;
  Here we entertain our friends;
Here it is we spend the years,
Here it is we shed our tears.

"Here is where our journeys start;
  Here is where our books are read;
Here's the haven of the heart;
  Here is where our prayers are said.
This is home, where all may see,
Just what we have dared to be."

ENGLISH MEMORY

Into an English churchyard with tombstones old
    and new
Time was my mother took me, as English mothers
    do.
Though I was but a youngster I still recall that
    she
Was proudly introducing the family's dead to me.

"Now here's your great grandfather," I still can hear
    her say.
"An upright man and stalwart and honored in his
    day.
And here's his elder brother beneath this grassy
    mound
He lived to five and eighty and owed no man a
    pound.

"Just yonder is your uncle! The family boasts in
    pride
The king himself came calling the day before he
    died."
Thus round about she led me, as now I still recall,
And read their names and told me the glories of
    them all.

'Tis strange that I've forgotten, I've been so long
    away,

The living English comrades with whom I used
to play;
The lanes, the homes, the gardens forgotten are
and yet
That little English churchyard I never can forget.

ஃ   ஃ   ஃ

"SHE"

In matters of gender my grandfather knew
Only two.
"It" was a pronoun he seemed to taboo,
But he leaned on the feminine all his life through.
He spoke of the watch in his pocket as "she,"
Never "he."
Did the hall clock stop running his comment would
be:
"I'll get her going! Just leave her to me."
Door locks and hinges and gadgets like these:
Floor lamps and keys;
All that could break, fall apart, burn or freeze
In the list of devices to grandpa were "she's."

And now though it's years since they called him
away,
I still hear him say:
"She's ready to go; you will find her okay!
She was broken down once but she's running today!"

BOYHOOD CODE

We had our woes and quarreled some.
  We shook our fists and shouted names,
But just as sure as day would come
  We'd all return to play our games.
We had our code of right and wrong,
  And what was mean and what was fair;
But nothing mattered very long,
  For boyhood had no time to spare.

The bully reigned his little while,
  Until some angry, plucky chap
Would turn on him in proper style,
  And give his ugly face a slap.
We formed a ring, they fought it out,
  And that would set the matter straight.
Next day 'twas thought no more about,
  For boyhood had no time for hate.

At times the parents foolishly,
  Betrayed by bruises, tears or cries,
Would take our quarrels seriously
  And try to black each other's eyes.
But long before their rage had cooled,
  They saw the youngsters friends once more,
With all their little interests pooled
  As happy as they were before.

Oh, what a mess of life is made
  By grown-ups, thinking to be wise;

By selfishness; by being afraid;
 By greed; by cunning tricks and lies;
By hatreds carried past their day;
 By adult love of fame and power!
Our boyhood had the better way
 When quarrels ended with the hour.

❧ ❧ ❧

AGE

That man is old, I think I'd say
 With all his courage spent
Who with his best of yesterday
 Sits down and is content.

THE CALL

Not for the few today
  Clear comes the call,
But near or far away
  For one and all.

Rich, poor, the great, the low,
  What road they fare,
Or to what church they go,
  What form the prayer;

Nothing now matters more.
  Naught's left to choose.
Dark lie the years before
  Should we refuse.

"Land of the Free," the song
  Sing as we go.
All, all one mighty throng
  Keeping it so!

Bright flag of stripe and star;
  Long may it wave!
Time now to prove we are
  Home of the brave!

DECEMBER 7, 1941

Never this date shall come again
  But Japanese must burn with shame
Nor all their shrines and Holy men
  Shall ever win them back to fame.

Long after peace is won and made
  And safety comes to land and sea
And present hatreds cool and fade
  Remembered still this day will be.

There have been villainies of yore.
  Vile deeds have stained men's book of years
But naught in all that's gone before
  So vile and foul as this appears.

December Seven! Oh, yellow race
  Your sons, their sons, nor all your kind
From memory can now erase
  The shame this date will call to mind.

December Seven! Now mark it well,
  This day will ever more proclaim
The crimes by which all Nippon fell
  Into the foulest depths of shame.

PRAYER FOR STRENGTH

Dear Lord, once more we face the tasks
Which righteousness of free men asks,
And once again for strength we pray
To do our duty, come what may.

Grant us the courage we shall need
For every sacrificial deed.
Till final victory we reach
Silence our tongues to careless speech.

Hearten us under flame and fire.
Grant patience to us when we tire.
Let no one's faith in victory dim
Though days ahead be dark and grim.

Lord God of men, once more we ask
For strength to do a mighty task.
Again the field for truth we take
And give ourselves for freedom's sake.

❧   ❧   ❧

THE BOY'S LETTER

The boy's on duty hour by hour.
    He watches somewhere on the coast
For yellow worshipers of power
    Who play the guest to slay the host.

And though we had not wished it so,
And prayed that it would never be
We're proud he had the strength to go
And share the fight for liberty.

His letters hold no trace of fear
"Don't worry," is his opening phrase
" 'Twill all be over in a year
And back I'll come to happier days."
How's that for optimistic youth?
How's that for faith in Yankee stuff?
God grant the lad has penned the truth—
A year of war is long enough!

Don't worry! Yankee shots go straight!
Don't worry! Yankee sights are true!
These Japs will learn the Yanks are great
Before this troubled year is through.
Don't worry! We've the ships, the men,
The courage, training and the skill
Quickly to do this job and then
Back to the desk and mine and mill.

The boy has got us boasting too,
"Don't worry, Flag," I sometimes say.
"We've got a son defending you
And you'll come safely through the fray."
Don't worry! Work and watch and wait,
Mothers and fathers near and far,
No foe will pass the Golden Gate
While guarding it our youngsters are.

41

HOW TO FEEL BETTER

Want to feel better? I'll give you the way:
That task you've neglected, get at it today!
That letter unwritten, that visit unpaid,
That failure to keep to a promise you made:
Get at them this minute and clear off your mind
And very much better you'll feel, you will find.

Want to feel better? I'll tell you just how
You can sit back in comfort a few hours from now
And glow with contentment and genuine pride,
Get rid of those duties which you've shoved aside.
Just clear off the desk of your mind once again
And you'll walk with the step of all light-hearted
    men.

Want to feel better? Go out of your way
To some one who's lonely, and do it today!
Forget the excuses so easy to find,
Get your heart lighter and clear off your mind.
Get free from regret which a death might reveal
And you'll be surprised how much better you'll feel.

❧   ❧   ❧

FLAG DAY

This day is Flag Day. Birthday of the stars,
And thirteen stripes, blood red and vestal white;
Banner of truth and justice and the right;

Symbol of faith in God, not warring Mars!
Emblem of all things cherished by mankind,
Heads high, hands clean, candor of heart and mind,
Home, with its laughter and its sorrow, dear,
The dignity of labor through the year;
Unhindered choice of creed and prayer for all;
Flag of the land which keeps no firing wall
Or steel barred cells for men who dare to think,
No pools of shame where scholarship must sink.
Flag of the nation where is play allowed,
Flag of a people happy, brave and proud,
Banner of laughter, dance and mirth and song,
Lord, to preserve it ever, make us strong!
Unite us, heart and mind and class and creed
In these dark days of freedom's bitterest need.
We are its last resource! God help us all
Lest we too late shall answer freedom's call
And from the skies our Starry Flag shall fall.

YANK

There's a twinkle in his eye and a jest upon his lip,
No matter where you find him, land or sky or battle-
ship.
He carries laughter with him, for it lightens duties
grim;
And wherever he is ordered all the girls will fall for
him.
He was born of gracious people; was an Epworth
Leaguer, too,
Or a C.Y.O., most likely, or a Baptist Y.P.U.

From the city, from the country? 'Twill be difficult
to tell,
Give a task to Yankee youngsters and they'll mostly
do it well.
Put the uniforms upon 'em and they'll swing along
the street
As like in song and laughter as the shoes upon their
feet.
But the Yankee soldier's different in a dozen ways or
more
From the soldier bred for Hitler or the pagan
warrior.

He is liberal with his money and he's generous with
his smokes,
And no matter where he hails from, he is fond of
drinking "cokes."
He's a "hot dog-hamburg" eater! He delights in
shooting craps,

But he'll prove a holy terror when they send him
    after Japs;
He's a gentleman off duty, but just let the fight begin
And they'll learn the Yankee soldier has his mind
    made up to win.

❧ ❧ ❧

THE TROUBLE

The Good Lord to an angel said:
    "Word comes to me,
The world is full of dismal dread.
    Go down and see!"

Back came the angel, swift as light,
    This word to bring:
"Lord, things upon the earth are right.
    'Tis now the spring!

"The grass is green; the skies are blue
    And every field,
Orchard and hillside will renew
    Their annual yield.

"Thy countless blessings, gracious Lord,
    Abundant, fall;
Yet men with cannon-fire and sword
    Destroy them all."

45

CHAMBERMAID—Name Fictitious

Before I joined the army and met Sergeant Bill
    McGee
The housework was for women-folks, or so it seemed
    to me.
I'd not the slightest notion in my young and foolish
    head
That any but the women-folk knew how to make a
    bed.
But mother, Sergeant William is as neat a chamber-
    maid
As ever cased a pillow or a blanket smoothly laid.

He comes in every morning and he looks about the
    room
Shouting: "Hey! Whoever learned you how to use
    a pan and broom?
Get busy with the duster! Get your stuff in order
    neat!
Don't ever let me catch you with a wrinkle in your
    sheet!"
In the art of doing housework he has many tricks to
    teach.
He is very trim and proper in all things excepting
    speech.

His voice "comes up like thunder out of China crost
    the bay!"
And he uses bits of language which no chambermaid
    should say,

48

But at last when war is over and the final Jap has fled
Thanks to tough old Sergeant William I'll know how
to make a bed.
And somehow I've got the notion that no man will
braver be,
When the fighting once gets going, than will Chambermaid McGee.

* * *

BOY IS IN THE ARMY

Boy is in the army!
  Mother once was sad.
Somehow or other
  I was rather glad.
Straighter than we made him
  Now he'll have to stand;
Readier to answer
  Duty's stern command.

Love gives up with wishing
  Lessons youth would learn.
Discipline is rigid.
  Army code is stern.

Now he'll gain a wisdom
  We could never teach,
And a strength of purpose
  We could never reach.

Mother wished deferment,
  Hoped they'd pass him by.
He—I'm proud to tell it—
  Said the year would fly.
Said that he'd be better
  When they turn him out;
Eyes a little brighter,
  Body straight and stout.

Now the worst is over,
  Parting pangs forgot.
Letters tell the army's
  Helping him a lot.
Mother's feeling better,
  As I thought she would;
Thinks the army training
  Must be very good.

FRIENDSHIP COURAGE

He never felt ashamed to say what many won't admit,
That he had seen another's work and highly valued it.
He never thought it silly to speak out a word of
cheer
While the one it might encourage was about where
he could hear.

When we called him sentimental in reply he often
said
He thought it rather futile sending roses to the dead;
And he thought it rather idle to be fond of someone
near,
And not say a word about it till you stood beside his
bier.

He wondered how the notion ever struck the human
mind
It was folly to be gracious and a weakness to be kind;
Why to dead men go the plaudits which the living
are denied.
And why fondness for another is a thing we ought
to hide?

All I know is this about him: Those he met along
his way

Found encouragement and comfort in the things he
    chose to say.
For the proof they had his friendship they were never
    forced to seek,
Since he'd told them so in praises he was not afraid
    to speak.

❦   ❦   ❦

THE CLASS OF '81

It isn't very pleasant, though I try to keep my grin,
To be told at every gateway by some guard: "You
    can't get in!"
To think and feel as thirty, but to have them say:
    "Begone!"
The minute that you tell them you were born in
    'eighty-one.

It isn't very pleasant by some youngster to be told,
When you're burning with ambition: "Sir, you're very
    much too old!
It's against the regulations. Stay at home and carry
    on!
We have no need of fellows who were born in 'eighty-
    one."

It isn't very pleasant when you're feeling fit and spry,
To have some desk-room major on your papers cast
    an eye;
And look above his glasses when the date he's come
    upon,
Saying: "Very sorry, grandpa, you were born in
    'eighty-one."

In 'ninety-seven they said it, with a "Hot Time" being
    sung;
They looked above their glasses and they murmured:
    "Much too young."
When the World War came I heard it, so of service
    I've had none,
Since I've always had to tell them I was born in
    'eighty-one.

ADVICE TO NEWLYWEDS

How to make a marriage go?
Well, the only way I know
Is to think through joy and care
Not as one, but as a pair;
And all matters to discuss
As they touch not "me" but "us."
Man and woman, heart and soul,
Holding "ours" to be the goal.

Ours the purpose, ours the plan,
One, the woman and the man,
Joined together, husband, wife,
In a partnership for life.
Ours the neighbors, ours the friends,
Never separate aims and ends;
But until all strength be gone,
One for both and both for one!

Who would keep the vows they swear
Must united stay through care,
And persistently remain
Wed in loss and wed in gain.
Doomed to failure they will be
Seeking pleasures separately.
These succeed and always will:
Joan and Darby, Jack and Jill.

These the pronouns: Us and We,
Very seldom I and Me.
Ours, for keeping eyes a-shine,
Is a better word than Mine.
Ours the plans and ours the dreams,
Ours the money-saving schemes,
Ours the single point of view
Holding us our lifetime through.

❧   ❧   ❧

MYSTERY

These wisps, so lifeless and so cold
Are seeds of last year's marigold
And each one in its little room
Holds next September's wealth of bloom.

PURPOSE

The first glad year we thought of things and gave our
hearts to stuff,
To find at last that ownership seemed, somehow, not
enough.
The garden was a pretty spot but still the place was
bare
Because there was no little child to scatter playthings
there.

We studied books on home affairs and followed many
a fad,
But still contentment failed to come with anything
we had.
There seemed no sense in beauty's wares or well
stocked cupboard shelves
So long as everything we gained was only for ourselves.

We needed dreams to carry on and hope's enticing
flame,
Some one beyond ourselves to serve, and then the
baby came!
Now Time is not an empty round which growing
boredom brings,
And there are pride and pleasure sweet and sense in
owning things.

FLAG DAY THOUGHT

Bayonets know no brotherhood,
 Cannon mouths repeat no creed.
Force and hate, however great,
 To destruction always lead.
High the flag of freedom holds
Dreams of all men in her folds.

Shackled serfs across the sea,
 Nations beaten and afraid
Trust their hopes of liberty
 To the pledge our fathers made.
Glorious flag of stripe and star,
Hope of all mankind you are!

Flag of all that men hold best,
 Flag which all, save tyrants, love;
Flag of truth and chance for youth,
 Flag of faith in God above.
Glorious flag without a stain,
Hearts and hands salute again!

ONLY THE VERY FEW

Were fame the needed thing,
  Then most of us have lost.
About life's circus ring
  At us no cheers are tossed.
The things we've learned to do
  Win never the encore's call.
Only the very few
  Gain plaudits after all.

Were wealth the thing to gain
  With shame we shall be met.
We've spent our years in vain
  And end our lives in debt.
For most of us, life through
  Earn merely wages small.
Only the very few
  Gain riches after all.

Were championships required
  Why were so many made
So quickly to grow tired,
  So gentle; so afraid?
All that we are and do
  Unnoticed seems to fall.
Only the very few
  Win prizes, after all.

There must be less than these
  Great goals, the Lord demands;
Tasks which are done with ease
  By friendly, eager hands;
Small glories to pursue
  For us who creep and crawl,
Only the very few
  Are mighty, after all.

THE ETERNAL STRUGGLE

The blundering ages roll along
Each one intent on righting wrong
And each one leaving in its flight
New wrongs for unborn men to right.

THE UNWRITTEN LAWS

These are the laws unwritten,
  The race's unprinted code.
Bite and you shall be bitten,
  Sow and you reap what's sowed.
Little is said about them,
  Obey them or disobey,
Believe in them now or doubt them,
  Whatever the cost you'll pay.

Courtesy's not demanded,
  Law cannot make you kind
Close fist or open handed,
  Narrow or broad of mind,
Needless it seems to tell you
  In matters like this you're free.
Judges cannot compel you
  Friendly and fair to be.

But as the seed the reaping,
  Just as the toil the wage,
Keep and the price of keeping
  Is a lonely and sad old age.
Smite and you will be smitten
  Smile and a smile you'll see.
These are the laws unwritten
  And never a man goes free.

GRACIOUSNESS

A quaint and gracious lady lives on a near-by street;
With smiles as bright as sunshine all passers-by she'll
 greet.
And if you pause a moment to say to her "Good
 Day!"
With some gay garden blossom she'll send you on
 your way.

From spring till late in autumn in bonnet and in
 shawl
You'll find her in her garden whene'er you go to call
And always when you leave her, whate'er the time
 of day,
She'll give to you at parting a delicate bouquet.

Her patch of ground is lovely with blossoms pink and
 blue,
In much the self-same fashion her life is lovely, too.
For never friend or stranger has tapped upon her
 door
But what the day seemed brighter than it had been
 before.

GOOD BUSINESS

If I possessed a shop or store,
I'd drive the grouches off my floor;
I'd never let some gloomy guy
Offend the folks who came to buy;
I'd never keep a boy or clerk
With mental toothache at his work,
Nor let a man who draws my pay
Drive customers of mine away.

I'd treat the man who takes my time
And spends a nickel or a dime
With courtesy and make him feel
That I was pleased to close the deal,
Because tomorrow, who can tell?
He may want stuff I have to sell,
And in that case then glad he'll be
To spend his dollars all with me.

The reason people pass one door
To patronize another store,
Is not because the busier place
Has better silks or gloves or lace,
Or cheaper prices, but it lies
In pleasant words and smiling eyes;
The only difference, I believe,
Is in the treatment folks receive.

It is good business to be fair,
To keep a bright and cheerful air
About the place, and not to show
Your customers how much you know;
Whatever any patron did
I'd try to keep my temper hid,
And never let him spread along
The word that I had done him wrong.

❧   ❧   ❧

A FRIEND

A friend is one who runs to share
Whatever burden's yours to bear,
And—a distinction rather nice—
Helps without giving good advice.

OVERALLS GRADUATES

I know Kettering and Knudsen, I know Keller,
    Zeder, Breer,
I knew Henry Ford back yonder as a light-plant en-
    gineer.
I'm a "knew him when" companion; one who fre-
    quently recalls,
That not one of those big brothers was too proud for
    overalls.
All the Fishers; all the leaders, all the motor pioneers
Worked at molds and lathes and benches when they
    started their careers.

Boy, that photograph of Knudsen in his evening
    clothes, today,
From a rugged suit of denim isn't thirty years away.
Kettering telling men of science what the green of
    grass controls
Worked for wages as a lineman, stretching wire on
    lofty poles.
Neither time nor strength was measured. Henry
    Ford went home at night
To spend hours upon his motor by a feeble kitchen
    light.

Keller, Zeder, Breer and others whom I could, but
    now won't name,

Had no high-falutin' notion ease and softness led to
fame.
They had work to do and did it! Did it bravely;
did it right,
Never thinking it important that their collars should
be white;
Never counted hours of labor; never wished the tasks
to cease,
And for years their good companions were those
brothers, dirt and grease.

Boy, this verse is fact, not fiction, all those fellows I
have named
Worked in overalls for wages and were never once
ashamed.
Dirt and grease were friends to go with; better friends
than linen white,
Better friends than ease and comfort, golf and
dancing every night.
Now in evening clothes you see them in the nation's
banquet halls,
But they earned the right to be there years ago in
overalls.

GREAT AND HUMBLE

One time I had the chance to stay
  Where famous people dwell,
And hearken in my eager way
  To all they had to tell.
But little else they talked about
  Than art and fleeting fame
And crowds, whene'er they ventured out,
  Who pleaded: "Sign your name."

At first I thought it fortunate
  On speaking terms to be
With human beings truly great
  The people flock to see;
But as the days went speeding by
  To my dismay I found
For earnest talk the proud and I
  Possessed no common ground.

Of fame few words had I to tell
  And none of art at all,
And coming out of glamour's spell
  I'd little to recall.
But there were others on the scene
  Who toiled with wheel and grip,
And I could chat with them and glean
  The joys of fellowship.

They talked about their children small

And summer gardens gay,
Of home and sheltering roof and wall
And all that fills the day.
They told of griefs they'd had to bear
As bravely as they could.
I left the great to take a chair
With men I understood.

❧   ❧   ❧

GROWTH

Patient on the parent tree
Ripe the fruit must wait to be,
So by processes as slow
Men in mind and spirit grow.

SELFISH CODE

Nothing matters more than you?
Try that for a month or two.

Center self in every deed,
Blind yourself to want and need.

First at table run to be.
Throw aside all courtesy.

When you reach the ticket gate,
Don't you get in line and wait;

Crowd in front of the parade,
That is if you're not afraid.

Push your theory to the end,
Pause for neither foe nor friend.

Nothing in the laws men write
Forces you to be polite.

It's your life you're living! True.
Try it for a month or two.

Try it till some passer-by,
Just as selfish, blacks your eye.

CHANGED MAN

I know he used to laugh at me
  And chuckle when I'd journeyed by,
To think that anyone could be
  So great and proud a fool as I.
"Babies are commonplace," he'd say,
  "And worldwide over they are known."
But he talks differently today.
  He has a baby of his own.

"Beware of him," he used to say.
  " 'Tis tedious stuff you'll hear him prate
He thinks his child superior clay.
  He calls his simplest action great.
I dodge him now whene'er I can
  To me a dreary bore he's grown!"
But now he is a different man.
  He has a baby of his own.

I know he tried to be polite.
  He praised the pictures I displayed,
But never thought it wholly right
  That such a show of pride I made
But now he boasts as once did I,
  And carries pictures to be shown.
He who once sneered in days gone by
  Now has a baby of his own.

GOOD NEWS

Pass up the war news and parleys on strikes,
Here's information which every one likes.
News most important; something to note,
Words with a chuckle and reason to gloat,
Right from headquarters I'm glad to relate:
Ellen Elizabeth's sitting up straight!

Here's something cheerful! News that will please!
Better than sinking of ships on the seas.
Brighter and lighter than stories of crime,
Here's happy gossip to fill up the time.
Born in September—four months to the date,
Ellen Elizabeth's sitting up straight!

What about Churchill and Hitler today?
Just at the moment there's nothing to say.
Talk of invasion somewhere and somehow.
That is a danger forgotten just now.
Here is my message, and isn't it great?
Ellen Elizabeth's sitting up straight!

Head on her shoulders and looking about,
Hearing our voices and searching us out.
Bright as a sunbeam and sharp as a spur,
All of her kinfolk just wild about her,
Grandpas and grandmas delighted to state:
Ellen Elizabeth's sitting up straight!

HOW TO BE HAPPY

How to be happy? Well, I don't know,
Since pleasures and sorrows come and go
And who this evening is forthright glad
Tomorrow with reason may wake up sad
And certainly, none for his little while
Of sorrow would call on the sad to smile
Nor ask so foolish and cruel a thing
As one with an aching heart to sing.

How to be happy? Well, I should say
Live to your best from day to day;
Think more of others and somewhat less
Of the loss and gain called selfishness;
Stand cheerfully to the weight of care
All shoulders and backs are made to bear
And carry about when the day is through
For the joy of others a jest or two.

How to be happy? It's give and take
And share a little of all you make.
Don't ask too much from your fellowman,
But grant him favors whenever you can.
Work hard; play fair; keep your conscience clear
And you'll be happy enough down here
At least as happy, it seems to me,
As ever a man was meant to be.

WHAT WINS

It's the everlasting climbing that gets you to the top,
And the everlasting sticking to the task you'd like to
drop,
      It's the grit and vim and muscle
      In the rough and tumble tussle
That will bring you home to victory and the distant
goal you seek;
      It's the ever up and working
      Never lying down and shirking
That eventually will land you on the mountain's
sunny peak.

It's the patient perseverance to the plan which you
have made
That will bring you through the dangers and the
pitfalls which are laid;
      It's the steady, constant driving
      To the goal for which you're striving,
Not the speed with which you travel, that will make
your victory sure;
      It's the everlasting gaining,
      Without whimpering or complaining
At the burdens you are bearing or the woes you
must endure.

It's the holding to a purpose, and the never giving in,

It's in cutting down the distance by the little that
    you win;
      It's the sure and firm endeavor,
      Not the brilliant stroke and clever,
That shall bring you home to gladness and to days
    of joy and song;
      It's the iron will to do it,
      And the steady sticking to it,
So whate'er your task, go to it! Keep your grit and
    plug along!

❧ ❧ ❧

LIFE AND DEATH

Remember when you're heavy tasked
  'Tis proof that still you live.
Dead men by none are ever asked
  To serve or lend or give.

HOME TOWN

This is the city called "mine"
  Where I know every spire,
  Can name pastor and priest at desire,
Know direction, device and design;
Have friendships deep rooted in years
  And memories tender and sweet,
Where against all life's failures and fears
  I have built a retreat.

This is the city I hold
  Above London or Paris or Rome,
  The city I think of as home!
To which I return from the cold
Of the strange and the far away place
  Where an alien am I
And no street or familiar face
  Ever catches the eye.

This is the city of all
  That is dearest to me;
  Where I'm happiest to be;
Where all things, the great and the small,
The streets and the buildings; the trees
  Have grown as I've grown,
Where whatever it is the eye sees
  I look on as my own.

MUCH OR LITTLE

If with little you can be
Glad the apple bloom to see;
Glad the wide world to explore
Riches could not give you more.

If with ordinary means
You delight in lovely scenes,
You will find your whole life through
Happiness abides in you.

If with much you still delight
In a clear and starry night
And a song bird singing near
You'll not long be saddened here.

Much or little, if you still
Look on childhood with a thrill,
And old friends rejoice to see
You will often happy be.

THE FROSTING DISH

A-licking of the frosting dish, time was I used to
    stand—
A pleasure, I suppose today, all youngsters still com-
    mand.
Not higher than the table at which the mother stood,
I waited for that feasting till she smiled and said I
    could.
And I had most forgotten that delight of baking day,
Until the grandson claimed it in the old familiar way.

The good old chocolate frosting—almost candy on
    the spoon!
Of all the joys of childhood, that's perhaps the
    sweetest boon.
And there he stood beside her as she spread it on the
    cake,
His mouth with that expression only appetite can
    make.
His eyes aglow with hunger as he voiced the ardent
    wish
His ma would hustle through it and give him the
    frosting dish.

I suppose since cooking started in the upward climb
    of man,
And use of fire was followed by the need for dish and
    pan;

Since sweets were first discovered and the women
    learned to bake,
And to keep the men folk happy fashioned pie and
    chocolate cake,
The happiest right of childhood and all youngsters'
    fondest wish
Has been the joy of licking off the frosting spoon
    and dish.

❧   ❧   ❧

WEIGHT GAINER

Bang on your platter
    And tinkle your glass!
Here is a matter
    Too joyful to pass!
Here is good news
    I am proud to relate:
Ellen Elizabeth's
    Gaining in weight!

Ellen Elizabeth's
    Added an ounce!

More of her daily
  To cuddle and bounce!
Hark to her grandpa,
  Who stops you to state:
Ellen Elizabeth's
  Gaining in weight!

Cheeks growing plumper
  And legs getting stout;
Isn't that something
  To babble about?
Draining her bottles
  At furious rate,
Ellen Elizabeth's
  Gaining in weight!

Cheer now for Ellen,
  Who's gaining in weight.
Twenty years later
  'Twill all be too late.
Twenty years later,
  As fat as a goose,
She'll go on a diet
  And want to reduce!

PAGING MR. McGREGOR

But she
    pered
"You wil
    I ge

As a tyr
Childre
    wa
At my
    gri
And t
    w
When
    t
They
    f

Say, Mr. McGregor, do still you go hoeing
That garden of yours when the green things are
    growing?
It's years since I gave up the glorious habit
Of reading of you and that bold Peter Rabbit,
But the son with your story who once went to bed to,
Now has a son of his own to be read to.

Say, Mr. McGregor—oh dreadful misgiving!
I hope you are still in the land of the living;
That while I've been delving in Tennyson's meter,
No evil has happened to you or to Peter;
That while I've been pondering Shelley and Brown-
    ing
You haven't met death via murder or drowning.

Say, Mr. McGregor—what's time to a story?
Only real people age and grow ugly and hoary,
But book-people live and keep on with their duty,
Grow younger and stronger and richer in beauty,
And surely while twenty-five years I've been aging
That foot race with Peter you've daily been staging.

Say, Mr. McGregor, I think it now fitting
To tell you the classics I'll shortly be quitting.
That now there's a grandson—a bright little beggar
Who'll soon want to hear about Mr. McGregor
And a grandpa about to resume his old habit
Of reading the story of young Peter Rabbit.

PLEA FOR STRENGTH

Lord, keep me working; keep me fit,
At windows I don't want to sit
Watching my fellows hurrying by,
Let me stay busy till I die.
Grant me the strength and breath and will
Some useful niche in life to fill;
A need to serve, a task to do.
Let me each morning rise anew
Eager and glad that I can bear
My portion of the morning's care.
Lord, I don't want to sit about
Broken and tired and all worn out,
Afraid of wind and rain and cold,
Let me stay busy when I'm old.
Although I walk at slower pace,
Still let me meet life, face to face!
Let me a garden plant and sow,
Set phlox and peony row on row;
Hew wood for winter's cosy fire
And at some useful labor tire.
This is my prayer: as time goes by,
Lord, keep me busy, till I die.

"GLAD I DID!"

"Wish I hadn't!" and "Glad I did!"
  Just like sunny and rainy weather,
Right and wrong, and sigh and song,
  Blunders and good works lumped together.

"Wish I hadn't!" how oft the cry
  Follows the pang of the moment heedless!
The good friend hurt by a greeting curt
  And the thoughtless jibe—and it all so needless.

But now and then there's a "Glad I did."
  A touch of pride through the spirit surging
A gracious deed in a time of need,
  In response to a vague, subconscious urging.

"Wish I hadn't!" is vain regret,
  A sense of shame for our blunders voicing,
But it happens, too, what is right, we do
  And "Glad I did!" is the heart rejoicing.

MOTHER AND A DOG

Mother insists we'll never have another.
  Dogs are a nuisance any way you view 'em;
The chores they bring comprise an endless bother
  And those who love 'em never want to do 'em.

Mother can't stand their yelping and their whining.
  She hates the feeling of their cold, wet noses.
In winter dogs tear out the sofa lining,
  In summer they dig up her garden roses.

Mother won't pet one. Not if we are looking!
  "There'd be no dog," says she, "if I had my way."
She can't abide their sniffing when she's cooking.
  She hates the way they act along the highway.

But mother always feeds him. If he's ailing
  She'll stand in tender ministry above him.
Not liking dogs, she'll give him care unfailing,
  Which isn't always true of us who love him.

❧ ❧ ❧

THE ETERNAL YOUNG

Little Miss Muffet is eating her whey,
  Little Jack Horner is thumbing his pie.

Happy and youthful as ever are they,
  Very much older and weathered am I.

The pieman of Simon his penny demands,
  Still after water are young Jack and Jill.
Though grandpa must do as the doctor commands,
  The nursery children are little folk still.

Little Boy Blue at the noon of the day
  Sleeps as of old by his tossed-aside horn.
And just as they were in the years far away,
  Are sheep in the meadow and cows in the corn.

The years, I confess, have played havoc with me,
  For many the changes that grown-ups attain;
But for the grandson who climbs on my knee
  The Mother Goose children gay-hearted remain.

SELF-DISCIPLINARIAN

I must get after me again.
    He's much too lazy and too stout;
And just to make the matter plain
    Comfort has almost knocked him out.
He's dodging duties he could do.
    He's staying much too long in bed.
And what with sorrow now I view
    He's thinking nothing lies ahead.

This fellow me is hating work
    Too often answering: "So what?"
Using the language of the shirk.
    I'd say he's slowing up a lot.
I think I'll have to discipline
    This aging chap to keep him fit.
This is no turtle race he's in!
    He needs to feel the whip a bit.

This fellow me would lag behind
    Without the driver known as I.
To indolence he's much inclined,
    He's over fond of cake and pie.
He's hard to handle; hard to train;
    Seeks always easy ways to win,
And since he's getting soft again,
    It's time he had some discipline.

OLD-FASHIONED

My old-fashioned father knew very few tricks;
He started at eight and he worked until six.
His ride on the trolley took almost an hour,
And longer if ever they ran out of power.
But he never complained or said things were all
    wrong;
Day in and day out he just plodded along.

My old-fashioned father was grateful and glad
That strength and clear head for his labors he had.
He used to remark, in a manner most grave:
"Man had two things to learn; how to work; how
    to save!
And what does it matter how long is the road
Or how heavy the weight if you've strength for
    the load?"

"Grow weary by doing," he frequently said.
"There's nothing like labor to soften the bed.
The pride of achievement by working is won:
You find it in hardship, but never in fun."
And my old-fashioned father went down to his grave
Believing he'd taught us to work and to save.

RULES FOR A LAWN

I could grow grass by being very stern.
   I could post signs *"Keep off!"* and *"Stay away!"*
The secret of a lawn's not hard to learn.
   You've but to stop the children at their play.
Seed well in springtime, water well 'til fall,
And block it off from youngsters playing ball.

The perfect lawn is beautiful to see.
   Grass well repays devotion, toil and care.
Top-dress it often, healthy it will be,
   But never let the children loiter there!
Don't let the postman cut a corner through.
Fence it from strangers, and from neighbors, too!

Rules for a lawn! I know them one and all.
   The first is guard it from the tramp of feet.
Fight weeds from springtime until freezing fall,
   And send the children playing on the street.
Post signs: *"Keep off!"* for all who chance to pass.
And by and by you'll have a patch of grass.

MORE PROGRESS

Sing if you will of the beauty of spring,
Sing of the birds and the pleasure they bring,
Sing of the hyacinth; sing of the rose!
Here is a song which I rise to propose;
Here is a song I am happy to pen;
Ellen Elizabeth's smiling at men!

Who can explain it and make it quite clear?
Still not quite ended the child's second year,
Still just a baby in bonnets and frocks,
One that her mother to Slumberland rocks,
Yet—and I grin as I write it again:
Ellen Elizabeth's smiling at men!

Gathering wisdom not taught at a school,
Knows men are simple and easy to fool;
Knows we give in when the women-folks fuss;
Knows there's a difference 'twixt females and us;
Knows how to work us and also just when:
Ellen Elizabeth's smiling at men!

Knows where the money is; knows where to go,
Certain of "yes" when the women say: "No!"
Not two years old and aware that we'll buy
Whatever she asks which the women deny.
What will she cost us at nine years or ten?
Ellen Elizabeth's smiling at men!

TRIUMPH

What on earth can be expected more of any man
than this
That his day should be deserving of his children's
welcoming kiss,
That his mind stay free from malice and his home
stay bright with cheer
And his neighbors give approval to his conduct
through the year?

Fame and fortune mean but little. Man may both
of them attain
And still be a fearful creature—selfish, cruel, sly and
vain.
While another not so grasping and content with
winnings small
May be everywhere respected and admired by one
and all.

It is difficult precisely here to judge another's worth.
Sometimes the richest spirits own the fewest goods
of earth
And sometimes the fattest purses and the fruitfulest
of lands
Fall by curious circumstances into most unworthy
hands.

So the final test of triumph doesn't lie in gain or
skill,

And it isn't strength of muscle and it isn't strength
    of will.
It's in something fine and tender by the soul of man
    possessed
Which achieves the admiration of the ones who know
    him best.

       ❦   ❦   ❦

THE BEST TEACHER

Old Failure is a teacher with no nonsense in his
    school,
No time has he to dally with the playboy or the
    fool.
He keeps his pupils toiling till they get their lessons
    learned,
And he tells them skill and knowledge are two gifts
    that must be earned.

Old Failure pampers no one and there's no one
    he prefers,

His discipline's impartial when some carelessness occurs.
The penalty's exacted from whoever it may be,
But he always rises wiser who is taught at Failure's knee.

By trial and by error and by effort down the years
Men are tested for their courage and by bitter doubts and fears.
For real conquests aren't permitted to the faint of heart and frail,
But are held for men of vision who are not afraid to fail.

The price of growth is struggle; true success is bought with pain.
Who seeks ultimate achievement finds it difficult to gain,
And who'd shape a better method than is known on earth today
Must have endless pluck and patience and through failure learn the way.

MOTHERHOOD

When in those well-remembered years
She saw her little child in tears,
She dropped all else in haste to go
To learn just what had hurt him so.

Today to him the thought occurs:
The pain she feared was his, not hers!
At her own stings of hurt she smiled,
But could not stand them in her child.

By day and night throughout the years
He was the source of all her fears.
Hurt was to her a terror grim
Only as it might come to him.

And so with mothers everywhere.
What falls to them they bravely bear,
Yet live in fear lest harm befall
Their children, whether grown or small.

THE OLD RAZOR STRAP

There was no safety razor in the days when I was
small;
Men used a thick old-fashioned blade or didn't
shave at all.
Then always on the bathroom door a two-inch strap
was hung
For sharpening the razor edge and sharpening the
young.
And when I needed punishment—a naughty little
chap—
My father thought it proper to apply that razor strap.

"It hurts me," muttered father, "more than you to
treat you so,
But this I do to train you in the way that you should
go.
Such dreadful misbehavior and such fearful temper
fits
Are proof you need some strapping just to sharpen
up your wits,
So come you to the woodshed. It is now my grave
concern
To give a wholesome lesson which you seem too
dull to learn."

The woodshed stands no longer, a garage is there
instead,

But there is no room for humans when the car is
    put to bed;
No space where son and father can in conference
    remain
And the boy acquire instruction at the bitter cost
    of pain.
And something more has vanished—is it progress
    or mishap—
On a hook within the bathroom there is now no
    razor strap.

In these days of great invention shingles, too, are
    hard to find.
There is little left to fathers who'd improve a youth-
    ful mind.
The safety razor's handy, the electric razor's here,
But for discipline they've nothing that a small boy
    has to fear.
Still, in retrospect, I'm grateful to that ancient razor
    strap
And the lessons that it taught me long ago at father's
    lap.

GRADUATION SPEECH

Said Old Crankmire as we chatted: "Here's the
    merry month of June
And the youth of school and college will be gradu-
    ating soon.
There'll be bigwigs talking to them. One old scholar
    that I know
Told a class room full of youngsters: 'To a troubled
    world you go!'
And for twenty tedious minutes he regretted and
    deplored
That the future stretched before them was with
    difficulty stored!"

Since that day I've often wondered, were I called
    upon to teach,
Just what counsel I should offer in my graduation
    speech.
I should not deplore the hardships which confronted
    them. Instead,
I'd congratulate the youngsters on the tasks which
    lie ahead.
"It's a troubled world," I'd tell them. "You will
    suffer many a blow—
You'll encounter difficulty, but be glad that this is so!

"I'd be very sorry for you were you doomed to
    easy years,

In a world completely finished where no need for
strength appears.
I should not congratulate you were you going out
today
All secure and all complacent with no barriers in
your way.
These are times of stress and trial and there's work
for you to do,
So set forth with hope and courage, for the world
has need of you.

"Ease and comfort call for little. Pleasure cannot
make you strong.
Pride is captured from achievement and from righting what is wrong.
Worth is only gained from struggle. Courage comes
from staying true,
Self-respect is wrought in hardship saying: 'This I
dare to do!'
So be glad the years before you heavy seem to be
with care.
'Tis a troubled world you're facing, but your chance
is waiting there."

OLD AND NEW CHURCH SUPPERS

We've been down to church for supper at its annual
    bazaar
And, somehow, I got to thinking just how different
    these things are.
They served us pan-fried chicken, with a salad green
    and red,
They had candles on the tables like a fancy banquet
    spread,
When I suddenly remembered (do such memories
    never fade?)
The supper of my boyhood by the church's Ladies'
    Aid.
There were just two famous dishes served in eigh-
    teen ninety-two,
And one was scalloped oysters and the other, oyster
    stew.

My father joked about it, as I'm sure did all the
    men,
For the males seemed disrespectful and irreverent
    even then.
Once I heard him call my mother just to whisper
    in her ear:
"There has been a dreadful blunder in the kitchen,
    Julie dear!
Do you think that it will matter? 'Twas a careless
    thing to do,

But I think you ought to know it—there's an oyster
in my stew!"
And those good old scalloped oysters! 'Twas his
notion that they ran
Five pounds of crumbled crackers to six oysters to
the pan.

Those old suppers of the parish! Oh, how swiftly
time moves on!
The devoted souls who served them to the other
world have gone
And our group, who were the children, are the elders
now who think
That the meat course must be chicken and the salad
green or pink.
It's to us they sell the tickets, it's by us the jokes
are made,
And the girls who were our sweethearts now comprise the Ladies' Aid.
But the spirit of the supper is the same our fathers
knew
When they dished out scalloped oysters or a bowl
of oyster stew.

MISTAKEN KINDNESS

I saw her sobbing 'neath a tree,
  "And what is wrong with you?" said I,
"So deep my father's love for me!"
  The troubled maiden made reply.

"So great his love for me, he fears
  To let me walk the street alone.
Never a task or care appears
  Which I'm allowed to call my own.

"Always his hand is at my arm;
  Secure and safe my life must be,
And since I run no risk of harm,
  Adventure is denied to me.

"I know he thinks 'tis love that makes
  So stout a wall 'gainst hurt and care,
But I would rather make mistakes
  And have my share of pain to bear."

PIONEERING

There's no sure and certain lane
Leading straight to fame and gain,
All is hazard; all is chance,
High adventure and romance.
But who wins, you may be sure,
Many hardships must endure.

Many failures lie behind
All discoveries men find;
All that scientists invent
Rises from discouragement.
Every pioneer has met
Disappointment, doubt and debt.

Luck? Yes, sometimes luck will aid
Men of patience, unafraid,
But it's powerless to supply
Help to men who never try.
All who prosper and advance
Work to give themselves a chance.

Back of every worth while gain
Lies the strength to stand the strain.
Failure, time and time, appears
To discourage pioneers,
But, until the day they die
Good men never cease to try.

MOTHER COUNSEL

'Twas thus the mother used to speak:
"My son, be gracious to the weak,
And never turn from need away
For fear you'll need yourself, some day."

'Twas this the mother used to tell:
"My son, go soon where sorrows dwell,
On earth the bitterest anguish known
Is sitting down to weep alone."

'Twas this the mother used to say:
"My son, be generous while you may,
For poverty's worst pang to bear
Is having nothing left to share."

'Twas thus, when I was at her knee
The gentle mother counseled me,
And now with shame my cheeks grow hot
To think how often I forgot.

THE FUTURE

Rough the path and steep the hill,
Step by step keep climbing still.
Wild the storm and dark the night,
Follow still faith's candle light;
Watch and work and wait and pray.
Little's settled in a day.

Look beyond the present fear.
Skies may soon begin to clear.
Burdens lighter are, you'll find,
Carried with a cheerful mind.
Time sweeps many a care away.
Little's settled in a day.

Nothing worth while comes with ease.
Hard to win are victories.
Who would skill and wisdom gain
Lives with weariness and pain,
Disappointment and delay.
Little's settled in a day.

Worried, fearful and perplexed,
Wondering what may happen next?
Brave the present moments through.
All tomorrow waits for you.
Work and wait; let come what may.
Little's settled in a day!

WORDS

Sometimes the words refuse to come at all
  As if from sadness they would keep away,
  Or wished awhile in idleness to stay,
Tired of some human's most persistent call.
Sometimes like soldiers into line they fall
  Ready for duty, be it what it may;
  Again like youngsters laughing at their play
They race the page, pursuing hoop or ball.

Words are the servants, and the master, thought.
  As all who serve compelled to "stand and wait."
Some into commonplaces shaped and wrought;
  Some made eternal by a craftsman great.
Words for man's thinking, swinging into line,
Waiting the splendor of the gift divine.

❧ ❧ ❧

BALLAD OF MAN'S LIFE

Look forward, never backward here.
  Tomorrow's promises are fair.
What if today is dark and drear?
  Little is permanent of care;
  Hold hope and throw away despair.

Although the end we cannot see,
  Believe in God, believe in prayer,
For all some purpose here must be.

God is not overly severe.
  He knows the weight our strength can bear;
Nor is He quick to frown or sneer.
  He asks that each shall do his share.
  Believe Him, weakness He will spare.
With this thought sages disagree,
  One deed may many wrongs repair.
For all some purpose here must be.

Oh, never look at life in fear!
  There's need about us everywhere,
Some one at hand or very near
  Whose day is dismal, bleak and bare.
  And if by chance we happen there,
God's right hand at the time are we.
  Born for that deed perhaps we were.
For all some purpose here must be.

L'ENVOI.

Dear Lord, these robes of flesh we wear
  At last will set the spirit free.
Yet whatsoever road we fare,
  For all some purpose here must be.

THE LIGHTHOUSE KEEPER WONDERS

"The light I've tended for forty years
Is now to be run by a set of gears,"
The keeper said, "and it isn't nice
To be put ashore by a mere device.
Now fair or foul the winds that blow
Or smooth or rough the sea below
It is all the same. The ships at night
Will run to an automatic light.

"That clock and gear which truly turn
Are timed and set so the light will burn,
But did ever an automatic thing
Set plants about in the early spring?
And did ever a bit of wire and gear
A cry for help in the darkness hear,
Or welcome callers and show them through
The lighthouse rooms as I used to do?

" 'Tis not in malice these things I say.
All men must bow to the newer way,
But it's strange for a lighthouse man like me
After forty years on shore to be.
And I wonder now will the grass stay green?
Will the brass stay bright and the windows clean,
And will ever that automatic thing
Plant marigold in the early spring?"

FISHING INCIDENT

Away from bench and lathe and steam
He went to wade a northern stream
And set his tired eyes to catch
The mystery of a summer hatch;
To try his wrist and learn if skill
Remained his proud possession still.

Hungry and tired, upon the shore
At noon he built a fire once more.
He boiled his coffee over wood;
Fried fish and found them very good.
A stranger passed with rod and line;
He promptly asked him in to dine.

They sat an hour and talked of flies,
To just what lure the trout would rise;
Where, when, by whom was made a catch
Which every angler hoped to match.
Until: "Well, let's be off again!
Remember, we are fishermen!"

Strange incident. To make it brief
One was a workman, one his chief.
One by a numbered badge was known
Which at the factory must be shown,
But both were fishing for the day
And which was which I couldn't say.

GOOD FRIDAY

This was the darkest day of all,
  When failure seemed His lot;
When Pilate in the council hall
  All else, but self, forgot
And, hearing angry crowds outside
  So frightened grew to be,
He sent Him to be crucified
  And set Barabbas free.

Barabbas, murderer and worse,
  Condemned by peers to die,
So runs the story, verse by verse.
  Was used his life to buy.
And when upon the Cross that day
  The gentle Christ was nailed,
And all His friends had run away,
  He wondered, had He failed?

For Him a crown of thorns was made
  And placed upon His head.
A jeering throng about Him stayed
  Until they thought Him dead.
And in the gloom of that last hour,
  So far as men could see,
The worshipers of wealth and power
  Triumphant seemed to be.

None knows where vile Barabbas fled
  Or what he lived to do.
No word of him has since been said
  By Gentile or by Jew.
But all men know the Christ they killed
  That day, in hate and shame,
And never will His voice be stilled
  Or men forget His name.

❧   ❧   ❧

RED CROSS

For just a few dollars——a ship far at sea
Will hasten to rescue the drowning—for me;
For just a few dollars flicked out of my purse
I can give to a soldier the care of a nurse.

THE INCOMPREHENSIBLE GARDEN

My garden plot, considered small,
Has room for morning glories tall,
A clump or two of sturdy phlox
And marigold and hollyhocks
Enough to occupy my mind
Forever were I so inclined.

Though small the space it holds for me
 An endless tale of mystery
And worlds most intricately planned
I shall not live to understand.
Even the magic of the rain
Works marvels I cannot explain.

Those few brave roses which I grow
Hold secrets I shall never know;
For though I spent all waking hours
In close communion with the flowers,
 I should not learn how white and red
Are fashioned in the self-same bed.

My garden opens to my eyes
The miracles of butterflies,
 And furnishes, the whole day long,
The rapture of exultant song.
Though small the plot, from end to end,
'Tis much too great to comprehend.

SIMPLE SPEECH

He chose the gentle words and small,
  The cheerful and the clean,
And seemed to guard his lips from all
  The cruel and the mean.

And if he thought a bitter thing,
  Or if a shame he knew;
From scandal's ever-growing ring
  He silently withdrew.

He talked in such a simple way
  That 'round the neighborhood
The children and the grown-ups gray
  His meaning understood.

And never sensing burn or sting,
  In time we came to see
How very beautiful a thing
  Such simple speech can be.

Seal the stone about his clay,
  'Grave it with his name;
Cut thereon his natal day;
  Tell when parting came;
Little stone can do or say
  To increase his fame.

Sleeping with the vicars there,
  Leave him now for aye!
Done with all the bitter care
  Of life's fretful day;
 Gone the crown of Christ to wear,
  With the saints to stay.

Deeper far than granite cold
  Hearts by love are stirred.
Longer, longer, they can hold
  Something faintly heard,
So upon our lives is scrolled:
  Peace, his final word.

LITTLE BOY IN THE COUNTRY

Last evening down the country lane
  They took me to a farmer's house
  To watch the women milk the cows
And drive them to field again.

And though I'm two years old and more,
  Since in the city I was born
  I'd never seen great bins of corn
Or stood so close to cows before.

They let me pat each slippery nose
  And stroke the coats as soft as silk.
  I watched the pails fill up with milk
And helped the man the gate to close.

Now I am back at home again,
  And wish that every boy like me
  So close sometime to cows could be
And walk behind them down a lane.

LIFE'S FINEST GIFTS

When you get "on" and you've lived a lot
And the blood in your veins isn't quite so hot,
Though your eyes are dimmer than what they were
And the page of the book has a misty blur,
Strange as the case may seem to be,
Then is the time you will clearly see.

You'll see yourself as you really are,
When you've lived a lot and you've traveled far,
When your strength gives out and your muscles tire
You'll see the folly of mad desire;
You'll see what now to your sight is hid,
The numberless trivial things you did.

Often the blindest are youthful eyes,
For age must come ere a man grows wise,
And youth makes much of the mountain peaks,
And the strife for fame and the goal it seeks,
But age sits down with the setting sun
And smiles at the boastful deeds it's done.

You'll sigh for the friends that were turned aside
By a hasty word or a show of pride,
You'll laugh at medals that now you prize,
For you'll look at them through clearer eyes
And see how little they really meant
For which so much of your strength was spent.

You'll see, as always an old man sees,
That the waves die down with the fading breeze,
That the pomps of life never last for long,
And the great sink back to the common throng,
And you'll understand when the struggle ends
That the finest gifts of this life are friends.

❧   ❧   ❧

ACHIEVEMENT

I passed his house just yesterday,
  And at the front gate chanced to see
In all its glorious display
  A blossoming magnolia tree.

I do not know the man at all,
  Or what his life, or what his place,
Or his achievements, great or small,
  I only know that work of grace.

I only know it must appear,
  Though all things else be lost in gloom,
'Tis something in a man's career
  To bring so fair a tree to bloom.

Against the wrong he may have done,
  The blundering of his mind and hands,
That burst of splendor in the sun
  Forever to his credit stands.

WOMAN'S WILE

In summing up my small affairs
I reckon in our flight of stairs
And always charge the sums they've cost
As money absolutely lost.
All down the years, both night and day
A double charge I've had to pay
For countless little things she wears
Because "she's left her purse upstairs!"

Long years ago a plan we made
Of bills which should by her be paid
And came by study to agree
On those which should be met by me.
Nor did I guess, so young was I,
How deep a woman's thoughts may lie.
This came upon me unawares:
"My dear, I've left my purse upstairs."

Her loss at bridge; the laundry bill,
For sweets the candy jar to fill;
For boys who peddle magazines,
And small repairs on house machines;
For tickets to the church bazaar
(These cash transactions always are)
I'm made to pay as she declares:
"My dear, I've left my purse upstairs."

FUTURE

If this be all the life we live,
　　If this be dream and end of dream
If life has nothing more to give
　　How futile faith and reason seem!

If nothing more awaits us all
　　Then thought is self-created pain,
And foolish are the tears that fall
　　And silly every counted gain.

'Twere better as the beasts to feed
　　And seek some sunny place to lie
Than trouble mind with code and creed
　　If as the beasts we merely die.

But something which we cannot prove
　　In any scientific way
Lifts us from instinct's settled groove
　　And causes us to think and pray.

And something which as faith we know
　　Keeps holding fast the thought in mind
That when from earth as souls we go
　　Some new experience we'll find.

MANHOOD

These things all men admire:
Real courage under fire;
Clean living; strength of will;
High faith, and hard-earned skill;
Soul's depth and breadth of mind;
The grace of being kind.

These things all men will praise:
Greatness with simple ways;
True sympathy which shows
Knowledge of hurts and woes;
Good nature that can wear
Under life's fretful care.

How in opinion climb?
How make the most of time?
How come to manhood's goal?
Work with both heart and soul,
Seeking again, again,
All that's admired by men.

Honor, temptation proved,
Faith steadfast, stanch, unmoved!
Speech gentle, thoughtful, kind;
These show the tolerant mind.
These since the race began
Always have marked the man!

NEANDERTHAL THINKING

Perhaps the man Neanderthal
Fancied his rocky cave was all;
That what he was allowed to see
Was all that here could ever be;
That man no more from life could gain
Than food and shelter from the rain.

He could not vision, nor could they
Who followed him long years away,
The ships, the trains, the cars, the gears,
That mark man's progress down the years.
Age after age has come, and each
Has thought no higher man could reach.

Not long ago, the midnight oil
Was symbol of a student's toil;
The pace of man from sun to sun,
The speed at which a horse could run.
And in the world our fathers knew
No one used radio or flew.

Who knows what wonders round us lie
Still hidden from the searching eye;
What marvels in the realm of thought
Stay waiting to be learned and wrought,
And who of us can truly say
What life shall be ten years away?

NIGHT GAME

Thought it couldn't happen; baseball seemed to me
Something for the sunshine, so the fans could see.
Read about them playing 'neath the stars at night,
Wondered how they ever watched the ball in flight.
Just a bit old-fashioned—fogey if you will—
Clinging to the notion things are standing still.

Thought they'd never do it. Baseball had to be
Played 'twixt noon and twilight. "Batter up!" at
    three.
Baseball needed sunshine; couldn't do with moon
All the games were scheduled for the afternoon.
'Twill be so forever! Age is seldom right!
Learned another lesson! Saw a game last night.

Went to see the Tigers play Chicago's Sox,
Stands were packed with people, Newsom in the
    box.
Field was brightly lighted—all as clear as day—
Even read the scoreboard five hundred feet away—
Thought 'twould never happen; sure they needed
    sun,
Fool am I for ever thinking "can't be done!"

AUTUMN

Autumn is a hazy time,
Some days a warm and lazy time
When everywhere you turn to look
The sumach seems on fire.
The hills and fields, about to rest,
The trees are closing at their best,
Which strikes me as the perfect way
For living things to tire.

In every landscape's gay design
There is a hint of power divine.
Sometimes a dwarfed and twisted tree
Is robed in richest gold
As if the Lord had said: "In spring
You will be bent with suffering,
But glow with beauty when at last
The year is growing old."

Autumn is the ending time
A bruise and heartache mending time,
When glory is awarded
Unto every plant and tree
And everything is at its best
In bronze and gold and scarlet dressed.
Oh, would it were that way with men
And could be so with me!

GROWTH AND PAIN

I don't know whether the stone can feel
The cutting edge of the chisel steel;
So still it stays that I cannot know
If pain is dealt by the mallet blow,
But this I know when the work is done,
By the cutting edge was the statue won.

I've wondered oft if the rose of June
Cries out in pain when I come to prune;
So still it stays 'neath the biting steel
That no man knows what a bush may feel,
But this unto gardeners all is known
'Tis by cutting back are roses grown.

And this I know and have wondered why:
Man's very first sound is an infant cry;
A boy is known by the pain he bears,
And a man by the way he shoulders cares;
The soul is shaped and a life made great
As the years go on by the blows of fate.

BROTHERHOOD OF LAUGHTER

Laughter saves the heart from breaking,
Keeps the tired flesh from aching.
Laughter makes the burdens lighter
And the eyes with twinkles brighter.

None while laughing can remember
Be this April or December.
No one in the joy of laughter
Thinks that grief may follow after.

Laughter, 'til what starts it passes,
Is a leveler of classes.
Who can think of power or money
Hearing, seeing something funny?

Solemn preachments oft divide us.
Selfish interests hard may ride us,
But when laughter is incited
All who share it are united.

WHY MEN PLAY GOLF

When the grass grows green again
Where the snow and ice have lain

And the birds begin to sing
Songs of welcome to the spring

Men will hasten to explain
Why they've turned to golf again.

Bankers proud will murmur this:
"Such a day's too rare to miss!"

Lawyers very grave and wise
Will profess 'tis exercise,

Saying, "better golf to play
Than have doctor's bills to pay.

Every afternoon out here
Lengthens life about a year."

If of parsons you inquire,
'Tis all nature they admire.

Golfers seldom will admit
That the ball they like to hit.

Higher far their motives run,
Golfers never play for fun!

NATURE'S MARVELS

By what imagination came
The rose's shape, the poppy's flame?
And who, in that dark earth below
Thought violets in the shade would grow?

Can anybody living tell
Who shaped the Canterbury bell,
Or had the genius to design
The lovely morning glory vine?

I know that things of wood and steel
The works of human hands reveal,
And round about me much I find
Created by the human mind.

But nothing man has ever made
Excels the peony's shape or shade,
Nor can the human mind conceive
Such mats as portulacas weave.

THE RUNNER-UP

If champion you should grow to be
Behind you, if you look, you'll see
One younger by a year or two
Heart-set on overtaking you.
At first you'll note him far away,
"A blunderer at the best," you'll say,
"And lacking skill," but look again:
You'll see him smarting under pain,
But trudging on, with stern set chin
To reach the day when he can win.
When next you turn, as turn you will,
You'll mark that youngster following still
And seeming, by this nearer view,
Stronger and somewhat cleverer, too.
No doubt as champion, for awhile
With tolerance on him you'll smile,
But if your pace one step you check
You'll feel his hot breath on your neck
And in that final, gruelling test
He'll pass you, bettering your best.
Oh, never yet was champion made
In any art or sport or trade
Who was not followed night and day
By one who'd take his crown away.

MOTHER DREAMS

The mother of a baby boy
  Has faith for every sorrow.
She walks with care to earn the joy
  That may be hers tomorrow.

With tenderness his hurts she'll cure
  Hope never once forsaking;
His every action leaves her sure
  A good man's in the making.

Her dreams are always of his worth,
  Dreams nothing ill can smother;
When fame shall recognize his worth
  She'll boast: "And I'm his mother!"

A mother visions night and day
  One glorious hour, which may be
When triumph comes and she can say
  "That great man was my baby!"

BLOSSOMING ORCHARDS

Apple and cherry come to bloom,
  And peach and lovely plum,
And like a spacious living room
  The orchards all become.
Now tired folks, like you and me,
  Go tip-toe round about
The old-time loveliness to see;
  Life would be drab without.

We've braved the rugged winter through,
  With all its grief and pain,
But now the skies are gentle blue,
  And sweet the winds again;
And, notwithstanding all the care,
  The madness and the gloom,
There's restful beauty everywhere—
  An orchard comes to bloom.

We leave the noisy world behind,
  Its cruelty and hate,
One soothing hour of peace to find
  Beyond the orchard gate.
And there, where petals pink and white
  Come gently drifting down,
We give ourselves to pure delight
  Not often found in town.

Tomorrow back to toil we'll go
  And back to loss and gain,
With all that weary mortals know
  Of fear and doubt and pain.
But where glad-hearted songsters sing
  From many a blossoming tree,
We learn how beautiful a thing
  An hour of life can be.

❧ ❧ ❧

LONE FISHERMAN

I watched him for an hour or more
A lonely figure far off shore
And wondered was it fish he sought
Or solitude and quiet thought.

STICK AROUND!

If the task is hard to do,
Stick around and see it through!
Work along! The truth of it:
You've not lost until you quit.
You've not failed until you say:
"I have done! That's all today.
Here I let my courage die!
Let some other fellow try!"

That is failure, if you ask.
That is giving up a task;
That's refusing self a chance
To achieve or to advance.
That's admission—plain enough—
That you haven't got the stuff,
That—to put the matter straight—
Sets you down as second-rate.

Stick around and stand the strain!
Bear the blows and brave the pain;
You may fail, but don't until
Spent are all your strength and skill.
Never use the quitter's cry:
"Let some other fellow try!"
Don't give up your chance to win.
Stick around through thick and thin!

THE FRIEND AWAY

There's a friend not here whom I needed so.
Now the roads seem dull where we used to go
And the lake and sky which were once so blue
Seem darkened today by a somber hue.

Time was I thought that the woods were all,
That beauty dwelt where the trees are tall;
That music lived in the wild birds' song
But my friend's away and I find I'm wrong.

Though all things near are green and gold
They lack the charm which they used to hold,
And the place seems lonely and chill and gray
And nothing's the same with my friend away.

THE HANDKERCHIEF CARRIER

Not mine to question ancient lore
    Or doubt the tales the Scriptures tell.
The ages that have gone before
    All had their share of ebb and swell
And fad and fashion, mood and whim,
    And much of habit still survives.
Old Solomon—I think of him—
    'Tis said he had three hundred wives.

Now I've one wife, one daughter fair,
    And subject to them both am I.
The wishes of that precious pair
    I never venture to deny,
But there's one little trick they play
    When I am near, to make it brief,
Always one comes to me to say:
    "Just let me have your handkerchief."

I am the handy boy about
    At dance, at dinner or at tea.
One or the other finds me out
    And begs a handkerchief from me.
The daughter, like the mother sweet,
    In many a solemn time of grief
Comes up to me on eager feet
    With: "Let me have your handkerchief."

Oh, how did Solomon contrive
    To carry linen for them all?
Three hundred of them—all alive—
    To get the sniffles and to bawl!
He must have had a mighty stock
    To keep so many noses prim
And care for all that wively flock
    Who begged a handkerchief from him.

❧　❧　❧

SIGN

I saw a flash of red today
    A flash of red a-bobbing;
And thinking, spring is on the way,
    It set my pulses throbbing.

"And did you go to England, and did you see the
    Tower,
Or walk through Shakespeare's garden and pluck a
    gilly flower?"
But when I say I didn't, or doing can't recall,
They tell me very sadly: "You missed the best of all!"

No matter where I journey, or be it east or west,
Somebody always questions: "And did you see its
    best?"
"Oh, did you quit the main way to find some
    waterfall?"
And when I say I didn't: "You missed the best
    of all!"

So filled this world with wonders which travelers
    long to see!
So many finding pleasures which don't appeal to me!
That wheresoe'er I wander 'mid mighty charms or
    small,
Some one is bound to tell me: "You missed the best
    of all!"

And when life's toil is ended and from this world
    I go,
Shall friendly angels question of what I've seen below

I fancy when I tell them of snow-capped mountains
   tall
They too will tell me sadly: "You missed the best
   of all!"

❧ ❧ ❧

NEED

I can thrust pomp and brilliance aside
   And all the glory of the boastful great;
Can turn my back upon all worldly pride,
   But not the hungry poor man at my gate.

I can refuse some rich man's proffered wine,
   His table set with costly glass and plate.
I can reject his plea with him to dine,
   But not that starving brother at my gate.

I can look out on victory's parade
   And stay aloof as conquerors ride in state,
But when some faltering fellow asks for aid
   I hasten, lest my service come too late.

AFTER KISSING

Lady, in the long ago
Kisses given didn't show.
In the chivalry of old
Kisses taken no man told.
But the lipstick print today
Gives the lady's kiss away,
So, lest all the neighbors scoff,
Kiss me, dear, but rub it off!

Fair ones do not leave me, please,
Looking like some skin disease.
When you've kissed me on the cheek
Rub away the tell-tale streak.
Cousin Jane and Sister Flo
Rub it off before you go.
Kiss me, dears, but don't forget
Beauty paint is always wet.

Never think that I object
To the joy of being "pecked."
Kiss me often as you can
And I'll be a happy man,
But before you leave me stop
This old grizzled face to mop.
Lest some evil thinker cough,
Kiss me, dear, but rub it off!

THE SPIRIT

What is this thing called spirit, which wears
  This indifferent garb of clay,
This similar pattern of shoddy that tears
  And eventually withers away?

What is it sets us to thinking and dreams
  And prompts us in moments of doubt,
Finds beauty in mountains and rivers and streams
  And wonders what God is about?

What are the men or the women we know?
  The sums of their thoughts and their deeds,
Or merely the flesh that is bruised by a blow
  And the voices repeating their creeds?

Is it the raiment we cherish as wise,
  Tender and gracious and good,
Or the spirit which strangely is hid from all eyes
  And never is quite understood?

MEMORIES

These are things that I remember from the years of
    long ago,
The journey to the coal shed through a lane of
    shoveled snow;
The wood fire in the kitchen where the mother
    used to bake;
The smell of bread in oven and her Sunday choco-
    late cake;
The window panes in winter thick with pictures
    worked in frost,
And a life-sized crayon portrait of an uncle that we
    lost.

The thick-leaved picture album with the velvet
    covers red
Which encased our fond relations, both the living
    and the dead;
The quaintly lettered sampler worked by mother
    when a girl
And the box which held her letters, with its lid inlaid
    with pearl;
The gas lights in the parlor, with glass globes around
    the jets
And the notion only sissies ever puffed on cigarets.

It seems strange how much has vanished that was
    commonplace back then,

The dim, secluded small room that was known as
   "father's den";
The cheery old baseburner and that wreath of im-
   mortelles,
And that curious thing some sailor had achieved
   with oyster shells.
Oh it seems to me my boyhood had more memories,
   somehow,
To be stored away and cherished than are given to
   youngsters now!

❧ ❧ ❧

LIFE

Life is a chance to know the spring,
   The summer, winter, fall,
Friendship and joys and griefs that sting
   And love that shares them all.

THE BEST OF LIFE

Out of the hours and days and weeks,
  Out of the flying years,
Out of the far goals which he seeks,
  His hurts, his doubts and fears,
Man takes, if but his work be true,
Shelter and food and friends a few.

Man knows his sorrows by their sting.
  Of loss he's soon advised,
But happiness—a different thing—
  Goes oft unrecognized.
Or thinking greater joys await,
He scorns the lesser, till too late.

Oh, whether rich or poor he be,
  Or much or little gains,
All-centered in his family
  His peace of mind remains.
And nothing's right when falls the gloam
At evening, save all's right at home!

And looking back across the years,
  Man soon or late will find,
Delight lies not in high careers,
  But deep in heart and mind.
All happiness begins and ends
With loved ones, shelter, fire and friends.

JULY 4

God looked down and said: "There must
Be one great nation I can trust;
One country, free from all the weight
Of ancient bitterness and hate
To hold secure on land and sea
The blessings of democracy.

"And such a country I will build,
A nation happy, brave, and skilled,
A land of worship; land of good,
Of friendship and of brotherhood,
And there a flag shall be unfurled
Betokening hope for all the world.

"There shall no tyrant force be raised!
No ruin follow men power-crazed.
There every eye that seeks shall see
The glories of democracy,
And while that starry flag shall fly
Man's liberty shall never die."

And now today we understand
Ours is that banner; ours that land
And ours that purpose! Let us then
At freedom's altar fires again
With patriot zeal our faith renew
To every task that we must do.

CHANCE

Things happen in the strangest way,
  And dull were life were this not so.
Remove the chance from every day,
  Let consequences plainly show,
And most of us would sit at home
  Afraid a single mile to roam.

A grain of dust, a wisp of straw,
  A vain attempt to stop a sneeze,
And Time has taken from the raw
  The stuff which fashions destinies.
Two people meet and none can say
  What follows centuries away.

The future's made of what's to be.
  The past what might have been contains,
Yet back and forth men never see
  To reckon rightly losses, gains.
But all adventure and romance
  Are seeded by the winds of chance.

THE MOTIVE

All this is what men work for,
  For what they fight and die:
A little place of simple grace,
  A garden 'neath the sky;
All things to which a woman clings,
  Of chinaware and glass,
And linen white and silver bright,
  And candlesticks of brass.

World over men and women
  For these spend all their years.
They give themselves to cupboard shelves
  And books and chandeliers;
And whether proud or modest
  Or more or less to claim
The joys and woes each circle knows
  Continue much the same.

'Tis birth and death and feasting
  And children off to school,
The church bells' chime and Christmas time
  And summer's swimming pool.
For this is why men battle
  And boys brave death at sea,
That great and low shall always know
  These joys of liberty.

THE EXECUTOR

I had a friend who died and he
On earth so loved and trusted me
That ere he quit this worldly shore
He made me his executor.

He tasked me through my natural life
To guard the interests of his wife;
To see that everything was done
Both for his daughter and his son.

I have his money to invest
And though I try my level best
To do that wisely, I'm advised,
My judgment oft is criticized.

His widow, once so calm and meek
Comes, hot with rage, three times a week
And rails at me, because I must
To keep my oath, appear unjust.

His children hate the sight of me,
Although their friend I've tried to be
And every relative declares
I interfere with his affairs.

Now when I die I'll never ask
A friend to carry such a task
I'll spare him all such anguish sore
And leave a hired executor.

❧   ❧   ❧

SONG

I stand and listen with delight
   To singing birds,
Their music has no need of trite
   And foolish words.

MOTHER PATIENCE

I must have been a plague to her in days of long ago,
Who wished so soon to learn the things she hoped
    I'd never know;
Who paid no heed of warnings grave she gave of
    dangers near,
But raced the street as boys will do, insisting
    naught's to fear.

How patient was the mother then, although I knew
    it not.
She held my hand and drew me back from many
    a danger spot.
But, oh, I was a willful lad—most boys are bound
    to be—
And there was much to marvel at I wanted so to
    see.

And there was oh so much to do, which boyhood
    labels fun,
I did not dare to walk or I would never get it done.
I had no time to stop and look and listen as they say,
So many were the joys to seize and oh so short the
    day.

I must have been a plague to her, and worried her
    a lot;
A heedless boy is hard to hold, but then I knew
    it not.
But now, too late, I understand —'tis written every-
    where—
How much of pain and doubt and dread all mothers
    have to bear.

             ❦   ❦   ❦

OLD-TIME PICTURES

We got them out the other night,
  Those pictures of our early years.
At me in trousers striped and tight
  They laughed themselves to tears.
At mother in her picture hat
Propped high by what was called a "rat"
  They stretched apart their ears.

At what had once appeared to me
  The loveliest of lovely brides
Those children fairly shook with glee
  And had to hold their sides.

Thought I, such rudeness to display,
As once my father used to say,
  I ought to tan their hides.

They laughed at my de Joinville tie
  And at my pearl gray derby hat.
They little guessed how proud was I
  The day I purchased that.
They laughed at mother's trailing skirt
Which hid her legs and swept up dirt
  And billowed when she sat.

But let 'em laugh! The day will be
  When their young brood will smile.
Their eyes will dance with joy to see
  What time can do to style.
And showing old-time photographs
They'll hear their children's hearty laughs
  In just a little while.

SUMMER STORM

Blue sky and blazing sun had grown
A form of suffering all their own
And had begun to taint the air
With mortal mutterings of despair.
Then came the storm clouds, thunder-voiced,
And we beheld them and rejoiced.

Rain which had fretted us in spring,
Was now a sweet, refreshing thing!
Gray, threatening clouds, so oft bewailed,
With shouts of joy were loudly hailed
And rich and poor and high and low
Rushed out to feel the west wind blow.

Were all things lovely; all tasks light
And were the skies forever bright;
Were never anguish or despair
Or pain or sorrow ours to bear,
From pleasure we should turn away
And beg to have our skies made gray.

GLASSES

Glasses, since first their use began,
Have stretched the reading life of man.
I mean, of course, the lenses wide
By which all type is magnified,
And not the kind with golden bows
Forever slipping from the nose,
And not the sort proud matrons get
Pronounced (and spelled, I think) lorgnette,
And not bi-focals all condemn
Until the eyes grow used to them.

Had spectacles not been designed,
At forty we'd be nearly blind.
At best the most of us would see
A blur where printing used to be.
And lucky he would be, indeed,
Who still, at forty-five, could read;
Whose arm was just the proper length
To suit his fading optic strength.
At fifty, numbers phone books yield
From most of us would be concealed.

Though night and morn, seven days a week,
My glasses I'm compelled to seek;
And never (so it seems to me)
I find them where I thought they'd be.
And much I see through fog is seen

Because I cannot keep them clean;
Though my bi-focals fool me still,
And I suspect they always will,
Glasses, since first their use began,
I hold man's greatest gift to man.

    ❧   ❧   ❧

SUNDIAL

The sundial in my garden shows
The time of day to phlox and rose
And singing bird and honey bee
And people, growing old, like me.

POWER

These things I know, for I have heard
The music of a cheering word,
And I have felt and understand
The pressure of a friendly hand;
And I have seen in sorrow's while
The glory of a gentle smile,
And learned through many a troubled hour
The magic of a single flower.

Not for all things is man endowed,
Not all the gifts to one allowed.
But power to comfort and to cheer
And rouse the faltering spirit here;
To stay the bitter tears which fall,
Has been bestowed on one and all.
All men unto life's journey's end
Possess the strength to play the friend.

These things I know and understand,
The pressure of a friendly hand,
And how the spirit can be stirred
By that and just one cheerful word;
Minds may have wisdom; hands have skill,
But hearts have strength that's greater still,
For they, when skill and wit are vain,
Encourage, comfort and sustain.

POKING THE FIRE

Of all the tasks about the place
  When winter comes to shut us in
There's one which constantly I race
  Against both old and young to win.
'Tis mine to do 'gainst all who try
  To gratify their own desire.
"Just sit you still," to them I cry.
  "I'll be the one to poke the fire!"

My father made us clear the way
  From mother down to sleeping dog.
"Move back a bit!" he used to say,
  "And give me room to stir the log."
As selfish he, so selfish I
  Jump for the rounded shield of wire.
"Move back a bit!" as he, I cry,
  "And give me room to poke the fire."

Something there is about it all
  Too difficult for words to tell,
But smouldering logs which twist and fall
  Work something like a magic spell,
And spark and flame and smoke combine
  In scenes of which I never tire.
So to the end I'll claim as mine
  The joyous right to poke the fire.

JOY OF ACTION

Time was I used to play the game, but now I keep
    the stand
To watch the ball being thrown about by many a
    younger hand.
Too short of wind, too slow of foot am I to run
    about.
The umpire, Time, beside the plate, has judged and
    called me "out."
But this I've learned, as all will learn, from conquest
    and defeat:
There's more of joy upon the field than on a grand-
    stand seat.

Spectators have their bits of thrill, but oldsters all
    report
The youngsters have the better gift. To them belongs
    the sport.
The books of yesterday are closed. The records filed
    away.
The joy is in the game itself for those who still can
    play.
And we who've had our times at bat now frequently
    repeat:
"We'd rather be upon the field than on a grand-
    stand seat."

Think not that I begrudge the boys their right to
action swift.
I want them to appreciate life's best and richest gift.
The health to play, the strength to run, the season's
times at bat!
There's nothing Age and Wealth can give that ever
equals that.
And I—a mere spectator now——still thinking victory sweet,
Would rather be upon the field than on a grand-
stand seat.

UNION

What fastens men together is never fire and steel,
But something very simple and likewise very real;
A common love of gardens and woods and fields
    and streams
And all the endless hopes and aims which fashion
    human dreams.

Men always band together for pride and pleasure's
    sake.
Love welds a stronger union than force can ever
    make.
The joys of home lie deeper than joys of pomp
    and power,
And nothing's so uncertain as despotism's hour.

Men join for mirth and music; for childhood's right
    to play,
For all the common pleasures together long they'll
    stay.
The simplest garden blossoms have more to sing
    their praise
Than all the shackled soldiers that tyranny can raise.

THE MOTHER

She seemed so frail; so tired at times, and yet
She dared to challenge every foe she met.

Alone she stood for what she thought was right;
For what seemed best she battled, day and night.

She fought dishonor, sacrilege, disgrace,
And all the cheap temptations youth must face;

Though frail her body seemed, her gallant heart
Fought single handed all the evils smart;

Conceit and cunning; shame and foolish pride
She met head high, face front and open-eyed.

She fought them off, the dangers great and small
And brought her children safely through them all.

LINES FOR INDEPENDENCE DAY

Fling Old Glory to the breezes on this holy day of
ours!
Let it wave in brave defiance of all mad, tyrannic
powers.
Let us give our hearts to freedom till this holiday be
gone,
Great and humble, man and toiler, Stars and Stripes
—and all as one!

Red and white and blue the colors! Red the blood
for freedom shed!
White the purity of purpose of the living and our
dead.
Blue for skies that bend above us, and our children
where they play.
Flag of liberty and justice, here at home and far
away!

Give Old Glory to the breezes over land and over
sea,
Let it ripple in defiance of all forms of tyranny.
For as long as men behold it bright and loving in
the skies,
They will know man's hope of freedom is a hope
that never dies!

THIS FOR US ALL

Oh, when the days grow warm again and buds
    begin to swell,
There will be those who cannot know—at Wake
    and Guam they fell,
There will be those who'll never hear the robin's
    song again;
They gave their lives to save such things for all their
    fellow men.

Oh, when the skies turn blue once more and blos-
    soms grace the trees,
There's many a lad will think of them while sailing
    southern seas;
And many a lad will note the time and tell his
    comrades near:
"It's spring again at home right now, and only war-
    time here."

Oh, when the grass turns green again and song is
    in the air,
There's many a lad will think of us while standing
    sentry there.
And high above on man-made wings there's many
    a lad will soar
And give his life that gardens small may bloom
    forevermore.

AFTER WAR

In those better days to be
When we've vanquished tyranny,
Off to school will children go,
Men will harvest what they sow,
Girls for husbands learn to cook,
Students ponder many a book
And the years of life be spent
In the way the Good Lord meant.

When the madness of the hour
And this foolish trust in power
Shall have passed and peace shall be,
Youth will dance as once did we.
Youth will dream and plan and hope
And with problems grave will cope,
Build and fashion and invent
In the way the Good Lord meant.

When peace comes again to earth
There'll be song and merry mirth.
Sleep will come to infant eyes,
To the mothers' lullabies.
Noisy boys will race about,
Stamp their feet and loudly shout
And grow up, as twigs are bent,
In the way the Good Lord meant.

There's no mystery in the plan
For the brotherhood of man.

Substitute for hatred's grip
Just the touch of fellowship.
In the joy of being free
Life, from birth to death, will be
Joys and sorrows truly blent
In the way the Good Lord meant.

❧ ❧ ❧

TOMORROW

*"Tomorrow we will have a better life and a
better world." Interview with Henry Ford.*

I like the way of Henry Ford
    Who turns his back upon the past
Tomorrow's goals to look toward;
    To faith in mortals holding fast.
"Tomorrow's world will better be
In many ways for all," says he.

"Tomorrow when the war is done
    And genius turns from cruel strife
'Twill solve the problems one by one
    Which means for all a better life.
Tomorrow—just beyond the night,—
Will see a dozen wrongs set right."

Tomorrow, richer than today
    And all the mornings come and gone!

Tomorrow, where new conquests stay
    For skill and pluck to come upon!
Tomorrow, rich with hope and vast,
Better than all the ages past!

Some sit with eyes upon the old
    Some fancy ancient times were best,
But men like Ford the east behold,
    Turning their backs upon the west
And in tomorrow's sunrise see
The better life that is to be.

  ✄ ✄ ✄

CHOICE

Twixt flatterer and critic, I
    Prefer to play the flatterer's part.
I'd rather comfort with a lie
    Than stick a knife into the heart.

UNCHANGEABLE

They say the world will never be the same.
      I hold it will;
That when the cannon mouths have ceased to flame
      And all is still
Mothers at night world-over will arise
And run to learn just why the baby cries.

A different world the sages say 'twill be
      When peace is won.
Things as they were again we'll never see,
      Says many a one,
But when the tyrant frets the world no more
Parents will teach their children, as before.

War ruins buildings and lays waste the towns
      And maims and kills.
Kings are defeated and give up their crowns,
      As gunfire wills,
But children still at night will kneel in prayer
And ask for blessing here and everywhere.

THE PIONEER

My son, if all men you would please
And live your term of life at ease;
If popular you wish to be,
A person all are glad to see,
Be very meek and do not look
Beyond the latest printed book.
From pioneering heartaches shrink
And never lie awake to think.

By custom most of us are curbed.
We do not like to be disturbed.
That two and two make four we know,
But past that have no wish to go.
We'd rather on old pathways stay
Than struggle for some better way.
We don't like thinkers who insist
On teaching us a truth we've missed.

But, son, if something urges you
To join the lonely, thinking few;
If far away you sometimes see
A way of life that ought to be
And cannot rest until you've moved
The race from ruts in which 'tis grooved,
Then shout and make your finding known,
But be prepared to stand alone.

Be firm! From scorn you mustn't shrink.
The many jibe at those who think.

Be brave! For brave that man must be
Who seeks to change society.
Old ways we love, and it is true
Not easily we'll turn to new.
Remember once the Master tried
And for His care was crucified.

❧ ❧ ❧

LABOR

Two traits there are which make men great
 And one of them is faith in God,
The other: willingness to wait,
 To work and patiently to plod.

Above all else that man acquires,
 His gold, his lands, his dinner plate,
Are courage for the furnace fires
 And willingness to work and wait.

The fortunes dead men leave behind,
 Like fruit from which the juice is dried,
Their sons and daughters swiftly find
 Are stripped of all achievement's pride.

By strength and skill is worth attained,
 By labor self-respect is won!
By faith nobility is gained,
 And pride by something useful done.

OWNERSHIP

A ring-necked pheasant brings his flock
  To feed on corn which I provide,
Thus adding to my little stock
  Of pleasures where I now abide.

And there are twenty quail or more,
  Who daily come with me to dine,
And, like a miser gloating o'er
  His gold, I proudly call them mine.

Within a cedar tree near by,
  Which from my window I can view,
Are nesting mourning doves and I
  List them among my assets, too.

At dawn a cardinal with song
  Delights his mate in yonder tree.
I wonder, can it be I'm wrong
  In saying all belong to me?

THE GREAT RIDDLE

If we could come to earth once more
  To walk again the path of life
  Beset with care and fear and strife,
Would we be wiser than before
  And 'scape the pits and snares about?
That's something many ponder o'er
  And none has worked the riddle out.

To us would some remembrance cling
  Of all the cruel lessons learned
  When from the highway we had turned,
Of folly's cost and failure's sting
  And vain regrets for deeds unkind?
And would we, thus remembering,
  Put all temptation out of mind?

Would twenty visitations here,
  And each of years, say, three score ten,
  Make saints of ordinary men,
Forever done with jibe and jeer
  And selfishness and bigot hates?
Or would our old faults reappear
  And all our various petty traits?

WINDOW PICTURES

Framed by my window all for me
  There stretches far a space of sky
  Where white clouds oft go drifting by
Or storms approaching I can see.

Again upon a summer's day
  I scan a field of lovely blue,
  All calm and restful to the view,
The clouds of turmoil put away.

The window frames and lets me see
  The four rich seasons as they pass;
  Behold the greening of the grass
And blossoms come to plant and tree.

All life and death is there to view,
  And every change from birth to age.
  Nature's own rotogravure page
My window shows the whole year through.

IN THE FUTURE

And if men shall be rich no more,
  And there shall be less time for play;
If all, as many did before,
  Shall harder work from day to day;
Will not the children dance and sing
  And women bake and sweep and sew,
And all the church and school bells ring
  As in the days of long ago?

So long as freedom still is ours,
  What else to come can change our lives?
The little yards will glow with flowers
  When winter leaves and spring arrives.
Perhaps we may have less to spend,
  But who can say that's wholly wrong?
Hard work may prove the better friend,
  And anyhow we'll get along!

So let's not fear what lies ahead,
  Nor dwell too long with dismal doubt.
With liberty we've naught to dread.
  We'll work the future problems out.
There'll still be home and church and school,
  And love and mirth and lilting song;
And freedom, under honest rule,
  And rich or poor, we'll get along.

QUESTION

While there is cancer to be cured
　And swamps to drain where vapors smother;
While there is pain to be endured,
　Why do men war on one another?

While schools need countless things today
　And hospitals for help are crying
Why do men toss their wealth away
　On plans for war and constant spying?

While there is blindness to be stayed
　And still through regions fever passes
Why should such triumphs be delayed
　While men are making poison gases?

So much to do, so much to learn,
　So little time for man or nation
Why should mankind one moment turn
　To spread despair and desolation?

LIFE'S RETURNS

"Life owes me life," one said
"And meat and bread;
Beauty and friendships, too;
Strength for the work I do."
Then sat him down to wait
'Till life should find his gate.

But Life went marching on
Till youth and strength were gone.
Friendship had long since fled
The begging hand outspread.
Beauty, disconsolate
Had withered by his gate.

Another said: "Each day
My debt to life I'll pay.
Some small return I'll make
For every hour I take.
With every hurt and blow
Stronger I'll try to grow."

His Life became a thing
As glorious as the spring,
Edged with achievement's gold
And friendships young and old.
Eyes bright and hearts elate
And beauty round the gate!

FRIENDS

Friends are strange. You've got to make them
   Long before the day you need them,
There are gifts which you must take them,
   Such as books and let them read them;
Flowers you've raised yourself, and maybe
Something pretty for the baby.

Friends aren't gathered in a minute
   For the time you long to see one.
Here's the fact and all that's in it:
   To have friends you've got to be one!
It's right now; not some tomorrow
Friends are gained to share your sorrow.

Friends are strange, howe'er you take them!
   Here's the gospel truth about them:
If you want them you must make them
   When you could get on without them.
This is fixed and naught can swerve it:
Who'd have friendship, must deserve it!

FIRST SNOWFALL

Soon will come the snow, and we
That day slower-paced will be.
Who is first to rise will find
All his pathways beauty-lined,
And will marvel in one night
There could grow so fair a sight.

In the city soon must fade
Beauty 'neath the heels of trade.
Workers first to hurry out
Plough and kick the snow about,
And the wheels of business tear
Furrows through it everywhere.

But beyond where country life
Suffers less from haste and strife,
Beauty lingers, near and far.
Hidden deep is every scar,
And the poorest stretch of space
Wears the master's touch of grace.

Would such snow could come to men
At the year's end now and then,
Covering all the scars of time
With a mantle so sublime;
Making all men fair to see,
Even as the humblest tree.

REPORTS ON THE SAME MAN

They knew him at a huge machine,
  A toiler shaping things of steel.
They badged him: "Number eight-seventeen,"
  And timed him at his noon-day meal.
Inspected, counted, checked and weighed
They listed every piece he'd made.

They knew him as a man they'd hired.
  They thought of him in terms like these:
"Good workman! Does the task required!
  Says little! Tries his best to please!
White! Married! Sober! Well-behaved"
And "has a little money saved!"

Thus was his record written down
  And kept with thousands like his own,
But on the distant edge of town
  For something different he was known.
There by his neighbors this was told:
"He grows our finest marigold."

SOME DAY

Some day, sometime, somehow
I'll do the things neglected now.
I'll write the letters long delayed.
I'll pay the calls I should have made.
That borrowed book I will return.
I'll save a part of what I earn.
All this I'll do—once more—I vow
Some day, sometime, somehow.

Some day, sometime, somehow
With less resentment will I bow
To duty, once I see it clear.
A straighter course I'll try to steer.
I will to all more gracious be;
More generous with what falls to me.
Deeper the fields I own I'll plough
Some day, sometime, somehow.

Some day, sometime, somehow,
(Why is it "then" and never "now?")
I'll do the put-off deeds each day,
What cheering thoughts I think I'll say,
And others then may glimpse in me
The man I've hoped and tried to be.
That is if Life will still allow
That some day unto me somehow.

SEE IT THROUGH

Something difficult to do,
  Something you would rather shun?
Set your chin and see it through,
  Work and wait until it's done.

Something terrible to face,
  Pride and honor bid you do?
Calm and steady at your place,
  Hold your ground and see it through.

Unto all come testing things,
  Trying hours to face or flee,
Then brave all the battle brings,
  For the betterment to be.

Something bitter-hard to do,
  Something you'd prefer to shun?
Set your chin and see it through.
  Get it over with and done!

FACT AND FANCY

The more that I learn of my Nellie the more it
    astonishes me;
She abandoned the dreams of her girlhood my life-
    time companion to be.

The years have been forty or nearly since vows to be
    partners we said,
But there's nothing about me whatever, like him she
    was hoping to wed.

Her dream man was strikingly handsome, broad-
    shouldered, fair-visaged and tall,
Well-mannered and graceful and clever, and I am not
    like that at all.

Sometimes she has glimpsed him in pictures. I've
    known as together we've sat
In the darkness my Nellie was wishing that she had
    a husband like that.

I'm short and I'm ugly and pudgy. I'm careless of
    manner and dress
And I often do that which I shouldn't. All faults
    I am quick to confess.

My Nellie is all that I dreamed of! Still lovely and
    fair as a rose!
It's I am the big disappointment! But that's how it
    frequently goes!

SEEING THE WORLD

They are living adventure and living great tales
  On the land, in the sky, on the sea,
They are marching and riding the earth's farthest
    trails,
  All for you and for me.
  And to set the world free.

Had you heard of the Solomon Islands before
  The Marines met the Japs?
Did New Guinea and Iceland mean anything more
  Than strange places on maps—
  Grass skirts and fur caps?

'Round the world they have gone! On the seven seas
  they sail—
  North, south, east and west,
Living daily what once was a magazine tale
  And mere fiction at best,
  Now with freedom their quest.

They have gone from their schools to strange places
  afar—
  Desert, jungle and shore,
And these peoples and countries, wherever they are,
  When the struggle is o'er
  Will be free ever more.

THE BOYS

I sing them all of land and sea
   Of cloud and starlit sky
Who in the cause of liberty
   Are unafraid to die;
Young lads of just a year ago,
   Who with a sheepish grin,
Came tapping at our doors to know
   Were our young daughters in.

The far Pacific knows them now.
   Australia sees them smile.
To heroes great they've grown, somehow,
   In such a little while.
High in the skies they rout the foe.
   In dangerous rolls they spin
Who rang our bell a year ago
   To ask: "Is Janet in?"

Now some go down in submarines
   To seek the wily Jap.
Far in the Arctic's frozen scenes
   Is many a bright-eyed chap,
But some will come to us no more
   (And sad it is to tell!)
Whom I have greeted at the door
   In answer to the bell.

Oh hearts, courageous, one and all,
   A hand I wave to you.

Here's hoping soon again you'll call
  As once you used to do.
God guard you on your grievous task,
  And when this war you win
May you come back to us to ask
  Are our young daughters in.

❧ ❧ ❧

THE NEED

A little faith when doubt is great
That right will triumph, soon or late;

A little courage, day by day,
When hard and dangerous seems the way;

A little wisdom to be sane
When fools and selfish men complain;

A little vision—just enough—
To glimpse the gold in coarser stuff

And past the difficulties see
The better life that is to be.

When millions of us these possess
God's cause is certain of success.

INDEX OF FIRST LINES

Index of First Lines

PAGE

Index of First Lines

Index of First Lines

Index of First Lines